Range of Voices

DATE DUE

Demco, Inc. 38-293

Range of Voices

A Collection of Contemporary Poets

EASTERN WASHINGTON UNIVERSITY PRESS
CHENEY AND SPOKANE, WASHINGTON

Cover and book design by Joelean Copeland

My thanks to Chris Howell for his faith in this project. I'd also like to thank Kristin Marshall, Rachel Wilson, Joelean Copeland, and Jason Van Loh for their help assembling the manuscript and gathering permissions. Most of all, I'd like to thank the poets whose work is included herein; their generosity has been an appreciated gift.

Library of Congress Cataloging-in-Publication Data

A range of voices : a collection of contemporary poets / Tod Marshall.
    p. cm.
  Companion book to: Range of the possible.
  ISBN 0-910055-93-9 (pbk.)
  1. American poetry--21st century. I. Marshall, Tod.
  PS617.R36 2005
  811'.608--dc22
                                         2005016514

Table of Contents

FOREWORD

1   KIM ADDONIZIO

8   LINDA BIERDS

16   GILLIAN CONOLEY

28   ROBERT HASS

36   BRENDA HILLMAN

46   EDWARD HIRSCH

54   CHRISTOPHER HOWELL

62   CLAUDIA KEELAN

74   YUSEF KOMUNYAKAA

82   DORIANNE LAUX

92   LI-YOUNG LEE

112   LAURA MULLEN

122   LUCIA PERILLO

132   BIN RAMKE

144   DONALD REVELL

158   DAVID ST. JOHN

164   DAVE SMITH

172   Nance Van Winckel

178   Carolyne Wright

190   Robert Wrigley

199   Acknowledgements

Foreword

Because anthologies are synecdochal—a part standing in for the whole—they are limited. However, such abbreviation damages only when it pretends comprehension; conceived as a supplement, this book offers no such pretension. As *Range of the Possible* offered representation of a cross-section of interviews with American poets born between 1941 and 1959, this anthology offers a cross-section of work by the poets I interviewed for that earlier collection. I hope that these selections from each of the poet's work—five poems—are representative yet substantive enough to encourage a reader to find the original books in which the poems were first published. I have tried to choose poems by the poets that speak to the varied poetics that the authors have pursued over the course of their careers or to select recent poetry that I find compelling. The choices that have been made for this anthology are mine, but I hope that a reader will explore further than this book: five poems can provide a start, but only through engagement with individual collections of poetry can the talents and complexities of these writers truly be measured.

And yet, in tandem with the interviews, the poems of *Range of Voices* provide a solid introduction to twenty important and divergent contemporary poets that illustrates some of the threads explored in our conversations and, more importantly, a partial glimpse of the vast landscape of contemporary American poetry.

Enjoy.

Tod Marshall, Winter 2004

Kim Addonizio

Kim Addonizio was born in 1954 in Washington, D.C. Her four books of poetry all articulate a unique vision rooted in stark worldliness yet driven by a lyrical desire to transcend this broken world. *The Philosopher's Club, Jimmy & Rita, Tell Me* (a finalist for the 2000 National Book Award), and *What Is This Thing Called Love* also exhibit a dynamic formal range; from variations on the sonnet to a muscular free verse line, Addonizio's formal repertoire is flexible and wide ranging. A recipient of National Endowment for the Arts and Guggenheim Fellowships, as well as many other awards, she lives in Oakland, CA and is online at http://addonizio. home.mindspring.com.

GRAVITY

Carrying my daughter to bed
I remember how light she once was,
no more than a husk in my arms.
There was a time I could not put her down,
so frantic was her crying if I tried
to pry her from me, so I held her
for hours at night, walking up and down the hall,
willing her to fall asleep. She'd grow quiet,
pressed against me, her small being alert
to each sound, the tension in my arms, she'd take
my nipple and gaze up at me,
blinking back fatigue she'd fight whatever terror
waited beyond my body in her dark crib. Now
that she's so heavy I stagger beneath her,
she slips easily from me, down
into her own dreaming. I stand over her bed,
fixed there like a second, dimmer star,
though the stars are not fixed: someone
once carried the weight of my life.

1994

THEM

That summer they had cars, soft roofs crumpling
over the back seats. Soft, too, the delicate fuzz
on their upper lips and the napes of their necks,
their uneven breath, their tongues tasting
of toothpaste. We stole the liquor
glowing in our parents' cabinets, poured it
over the cool cubes of ice with their hollows
at each end, as though a thumb had pressed
into them. The boys rose, dripping, from long
blue pools, the water slick on their backs
and bellies, a sugary glaze; they sat easily on high
lifeguard chairs, eyes hidden by shades,
or came up behind us to grab the fat we hated
around our waists. For us it was the chaos
of makeup on a bureau, the clothes we tried on
and on, the bras they unhooked, pushed
up, and when they moved their hard
hidden cocks against us we were always
princesses, our legs locked. By then we knew
they would come, climb the tower, slay anything
to get to us. We knew we had what they wanted:
the breasts, the thighs, the damp hairs pressed flat
under our panties. All they asked was that we let them
take it. They would draw it out of us like
sticky taffy, thinner and thinner until it snapped
and they had it. And we would grow up
with that lack, until we learned how to
name it, how to look in their eyes and see nothing
we had not given them; and we could still
have it, we could reach right down into their
bodies and steal it back.

1994

BEER. MILK. THE DOG. MY OLD MAN.

My old man used to take the dog
out to the garage
where the poker game was
and set down a bowl
of beer, that's the kind of thing
he thought was funny. He used to
give me some too and laugh when I
threw up or fell over
a chair. He taught me to fight
by smacking the side of my head
with his open hand, calling me
a pussy. Don't let them give you
any shit he said. When he smacked
my mother she didn't hit back,
just yelled at him. Once she threw
a glass of milk at his head.
It hit the wall and broke
to pieces on the floor.

I was ten when he died.
Too young to figure it out.
What I thought about was the milk
on the kitchen floor that time,
how they'd both
left it there and gone to bed.
The dog got to it and swallowed glass.
My mother said the dog
just got sick. The milk
evaporated she said.
Meaning it just
went into the air.
I thought how could something
be there and then not. Milk.
The dog. My old man. He loved
a cold beer. Sometimes I'd sit up

at night in the garage and watch
how he drank it, tipping his head
way back, and I'd try to drink mine
exactly the same,
but quietly, so he wouldn't notice
and send me away.

1997

PRAYER

Sometimes, when we're lying after love,
I look at you and see your body's future
of lying beneath the earth; putting the heel
of my hand against your rib I feel how faint
and far away the heartbeat is. I rest
my cheek against your left nipple and listen
to the surge of blood, seeing your life splashed out,
filmy water hurled from a pot
onto dry grass. And I want to be pressed
deep into the bed and covered over,
the way a seed is pressed into a hole,
the dirt tamped down with a trowel.
I want to be a failed seed, the kind
that doesn't grow, that doesn't know it's meant to.
I want to lie here without moving, lifeless
as an animal that's slaughtered, its blood smeared
on a doorpost, I want death to take me if it
has to, to spare you, I want it to pass over.

2000

NIGHT OF THE LIVING, NIGHT OF THE DEAD

When the dead rise in movies they're hideous
and slow. They stagger uphill toward the farmhouse
like drunks headed home from the bar.
Maybe they only want to lie down inside
while some rooms spins around them, maybe that's why
they bang on the windows while the living
hammer up boards and count out shotgun shells.
The living have plans: to get to the pickup parked
in the yard, to drive like hell to the next town.
The dead with their leaky brains,
their dangling limbs and ruptured hearts,
are sick of all that. They'd rather stumble
blind through the field until they collide
with a tree, or fall through a doorway
like they're the door itself, sprung from its hinges
and slammed flat on the linoleum. That's the life
for a dead person: *wham, wham, wham*
until you forget your name, your own stinking
face, the reason you jolted awake
in the first place. Why are you here,
whatever were you hoping as you lay
in your casket like a dumb clarinet?
You know better now. The soundtrack's depressing
and the living hate your guts. Come closer
and they'll show you how much. *Wham, wham, wham,*
you're killed again. Thank God this time
they're burning your body, thank God
it can't drag you around anymore
except in nightmares, late-night reruns
where you lift up the lid, and crawl out
once more, and start up the hill toward the house.

2000

Linda Bierds

Linda Bierds was born in Wilmington, Delaware, in 1945. The author of seven books of poetry, including *The Ghost Trio, The Profile Makers, The Seconds* and, most recently, *First Hand*. Bierds is a meticulous crafter of her highly original work. Working line by line and never shaping more than a single poem at a time, Bierds has written an enduring and highly acclaimed body of poetry. The recipient of numerous awards, including the distinction of a MacArthur Fellowship, Bierds' poetry frequently calls upon both well-known and obscure historical figures and events to propel her work. Bierds is currently a professor of creative writing at the University of Washington.

Ritual for the Dead, Lake Sakami, Quebec, 1980

The moose has fallen smoothly, without sound,
lifting her head only once
from a tangle of sweet-grass and snow.
Now the Cree lower their greased rifles.
Kneeling against the cold, they open the stomach,
the tendons and black muscles, and now
two calves are peeled from the steaming womb:

> Their skulls are heavy. Their thin bodies
> glisten. They lie in the snow
> like the parallel arms of a child.

Slowly, two flaps of meat are sliced
from the mother's flank. The mouths
of the calves are opened. Now the salty flaps
ooze in their jaws like tongues. And now,
through the cold palms of the hunters,
through their stroking, shivering voices,
the dead throats are stirring,
the stomachs and hearts are stirring
the brains are stirring
as they glaze through the dim eyes:

> *This is the promise of sunrise,*
> *of harvest, of winter*
> *cracking from our tight bellies.*
> *This is the promise of blood.*
> *Swallow.*

1985

The Stillness, The Dancing

> *I am indefinitely capable of wonder.*
> —*Federico Fellini*

Long ago, in the forests of southern Europe,
just south of Macon, a woman died in childbirth.
She was taken, by custom, to the small slate
lip of the mountain. Legs bound at the knees
she was left facing west, thick with her still child.

Century by century, nothing disturbed them

so that now
the bones of the woman cup the small bones
of the child: the globe of its head angled
there, in the paddle and stem of her hips.

It is winter, just after midday. Slowly,
shudder by civilized shudder, a train slips over
the mountain, reveals to its weary riders

something white, then again, something
white at the side of the eye. They straighten,
place their lips to the glass, and there, far
below, this delicate, bleached pattern,
like the spokes of a bamboo cage.

What, someone whispers, and What, What,
word after word bouncing back from its blossom
of vapor, the woman and child appearing,
disappearing, as the train slips down through the alders—
until they are brands on the eyelid, until they are
stories, until, thick-soled and silent,
each rider squats with a blessing of ocher.

*

And so there are stories. Mortar. A little stratum
under the toenails. A train descends from a mountain,
levels out, circles a field where a team of actors
mimics a picnic. The billowing children.
On the table, fruit, a great calabash of chilled fish.
And over it all, a beloved uncle, long mad,
sits in the crotch of an oak tree.

He hears to his right, the compressed blare
of a whistle—each sound wave approaching shorter, shorter,
like the words on a window, then just as the engine passes,
the long playing out.
He smiles as the blare seeps over
the actors, the pasture, the village

where now, in the haze of a sudden snowfall,
a film crew, dressed for a picnic, coaxes a peacock
to the chilled street. Six men on their knees
chirruping, laughing, snow lifting in puffs
from the spotlights. And the peacock,
shanks and yellow spurs high-stepping, high-stepping,
slowly unfolds its breathless fan, displays
to a clamor of boxcars, club cars—

where riders, excited,
traveling for miles with an eyeful of bones
see now their reversal.

In an ecstasy of color the peacock dips,
revolves to the slow train:
each rider pressed to a window,
each round face courted in turn.

1988

MEMENTO OF THE HOURS

First the path stones, then the shadow,
then, in a circuit of gorse and mint,
the room with a brook running under it.
It freshened the milk, the cream that grew
in its flat habit a shallow lacquer,
a veil I tested on slow afternoons
with a speckle of pepper.

There was butter, cheddar, the waxy pleats
of squash, green as a storm pond.
Walnuts. Three families of apple,
each with its circle of core fringe.
And the sheen on the walls
was perpetual, like the sheen
on the human body.

My mother would sit with me there,
her drawstring reticule
convex with scent jars and marzipan, the burled
shapes of the hidden. Once she brought her cut
flowers to chill until evening, and told me
the mouths of the bluebells
gave from their nectar a syrup elixir.

It holds in suspension the voices of choirboys,
she said. A dram of postponement.
And I felt as she spoke their presence
among us: the hum
of the brook just under our feet,
the mineral hush of the plenitude,
then the blackened robes of the blackberry vines
gradually filling the door.

1994

SAFE

Safe, we thought.
The flood waters nestled
the arc of their udders, but no higher,
dewlaps, flanks, even the tips of the briskets,
dry. All day they stood
in the seascape meadow,
their square heads turned from the wind.
By evening they were dead.
Chill, we learned, not drowning,
killed them—the milk vein
thick on the floor of the chest
filling with cold, stunning the heart,
We had entered the house, where silt water
sketched on the walls and doorways
a single age-ring. When we looked back
they had fallen, only the crests of their bodies
breaking the waterline. I remember
the wind and a passive light,
then the jabber of black grackles
riding each shoulder's upturned blade.

1997

THE SECONDS

With a flurry of sidestrokes, the March wind
swims down the chimney, its air chafed
by hearth smoke and bacon. It is sunset,

and high on the inglenook shelf,
a gauze of crystal flutes
captures the lamplight. I am their maker—Laurent—
eased back in a soft chair, listening

to hearth logs sag through the andirons.
And thinking of seconds—first time, of course, then
the hapless devoted who step from behind
with their handkerchiefs and swords, ready to give shape
to another's passion, as a body gives shape to a soul.

When the handkerchief crosses the damp grass,
they must wish it all back, the seconds:
that the handkerchief rise,
flap back to the hand, and the passion
pull back to its source, as the sword and the pistol
pull back to their sheaths.
Then everything silent, drawn by some vast,
improbable vacuum—
as an orchestra of ear trumpets might silence a room!

Now the wall clock taps. Across my knees
the house cat casts her rhythmic thrum.
Once I lifted a flute, some second
blemished by a loll in lime, and blew
through its crystal body a column of pipe smoke.
I remember its hover just over my chest,
a feral cloud
drawn down and bordered, it seemed
in that evening light, not by glass
but by itself.

Seconds and smoke…
Into what shape will our shapelessness flow?

Outside my window,
two children bob in the late night,
walking with their mother on the furrowed fields.
They love how their shadows
are sliced by the troughs—how, over the turned rows,

their darkened, elongated shapes
rush just ahead in segments, waving
their fractured sleeves. Now their mother
is laughing, lifting her arms and pale boot,
watching her sliced and rippled

shadow—whose parallel is earth, not she,
whose shape is taken not by her, but the cyclic light

her shape displaces. Now her head,
now her shoulder,
now the drop of her long coat

have stretched to some infinite black bay
pierced by the strokes of a black swan.

2001

Gillian Conoley

Gillian Conoley was born in 1955 in Taylor, Texas. The author of seven books of poetry, including _Some Gangster Pain, Tall Stranger, Beckon, Lovers in the Used World_, and, most recently, _Profane Halo_, Conoley is a writer engaged with exploring where formal conventions, traditional structures, and language itself break down—leaving a reader with a poetry resolutely opposed to easy categorizing. A graduate of the MFA program at the University of Massachusetts, Conoley's work as poet, editor of the independent literary journal _Volt_, and creative writing teacher have put her in the position of observing contemporary American writing from a variety of perspectives. The recipient of numerous awards, including the Jerome J. Shestack award in Poetry from The American Poetry Review, several Pushcart Prizes, and a nomination for the National Book Critics' Circle Award, Conoley is Poet-in-Residence and Professor at Sonoma State University in California.

BEAUTY AND THE BEAST

That the transaction would end.

That the rose would open
            (her appearance in a Cyrillic blouse),

leaving the sense
that one had reached for it—

dust gray blue green manifold red and torn,
            his studied performance of a romantic mood.

He is still eating other small beasts.

She is sleeping alone
coiffed in the pleated moments,

only rising to bathe before the mirror
with its grand so what.

But we who have held the book with both hands
and let the syntax shape us

we are not evermore
as mirror or sleep.

In our modern cloven space
events dissolve to the sexual instant,

each of us holding the hairy hand
with thrilling lucidity.

So we never find out what we mean
but it flakes off on our hands,

so the pleasures we most desire
go unexpressed,

people of the future will also have

light, fragile conversation
and a hidden cottage with shutters carved,

where each summer we return
with no misgivings, no spectacle—

Nothing to be afraid of.

Only the 16th century air,
making it impossible to breathe more purely.

And she is femaling him.
And he is maling her.

And someone says, the end.
And someone says,

no, this is my body.

NEW

I says oh Jesus, can't I count on you people?

A zone goes   where sky's gone
what fresh hell for

burning and dodging , earth

more placid
where the state need not borrow. Have you seen the flowers on the river?

There is more to press them to, more

to compare. One has to swim through to find

this one   who had little to speak of.

This one who lay down though a motorcade went by.

Language of the west, please do run out into the ocean.

The art set crushed the tastemakers shamed Authority's myth layed out
    under a giant work light—

grid beware

the pile driving,

pile driving its two notes unevenly.

Some breeze   light rock in the kitchen   the dead crying not to be alive.

Human and elegant great structures Time glued,

one is seeing through slats as one

is ferried down Lethe, to green and neutral green, white trees, the dead

Why

at the beginning of the question. One

doesn't come home one wakens

Persephone to ask, have you seen

the daughters of Memory? Paper

is ash, eternity takes tumbling bodies into the apartness

One is turning away

Zero has a glade

One is a fiction

One is slow in the death

One dies out over you,

arm back in curved light

One is arcing back

One is not a fiction

Zero has a glade

AFTER

The composition was shy.
In the finished garden the corn and basil, fragrances mixing

in the humid chlorophyll,
the shaved grass full of dots and cells

as under the microscope. You slept backwards
that night, death in the portraits,

death in the tea,
death in the French doors—

And like him you woke
backwards, like a being in the texts

who gets to go back and forth
or around in both worlds.

Only you were still breathing in the house of flowers,
the lilacs at their time of perfection, pining visibly—

And a man was traveling,
giving swell to the cloud

among people whose souls were already mature,
among those who were just forming,

while you found there was no way out of here,
some street to flee down, some room on the top floor to hide in,

and as though without strength
or means to venture

(the mockingbird, the grackle in tatters
and their *caw, caw* at the trash men lifting a branch),

stepped among what
had not been transformed...

Sandals on the deck,
              the shine in matter—

1996

As in the Small Gaps Between Minutes

Under the non-moon, in the watery tint

of the nearly finished, the about to become,

the woman lies on her right side,

with her too many darknesses and their daily wars,

she lays on her back

wrapped in the long changes, the body inside her

upside down and curled into a seed—

Who feels at home in the family?

Wind that spat into a candle.

You who are clarity, you whose eyes

draw the soul like a pail of water,

as the most stormy of us respond.

With each pain the woman braces herself,

the soul readies,

the separate selves are sheared away—

Eunice, Matilda, Helen, Ethel…

the lazy teen, the eros of a dress, all shadows

darkening further, then

gone, outdated like doomed languages—

even the new woman, shoulder-hard, standing in the future

she had not thought to build—

As in the small gaps between minutes

there is no end

to the falling in love,

new lovers come to sit on boulevards

and the woman waits

for the body to unfurl.

One bee turned wild buzzes on the long thread
of late sun.

Juncos strike

at the millet, color almost lost in haze.

Not just nature as the mother anymore

but the fear of the other, of being

near— and the soul hesitates—

1996

THE WORLD

It was just a gas station. It was not spectacular carnage.

A woman in the parking lot, red I Love Lucy kerchief, dousing his shirts
  with lighter fluid,

a great love and a paranormal morning.

In the far fields   the aliens arriving, switching off the ignition,

new crisp list of abductees   though the closest we get is the radio.

Cool gray summer morning the first heat making an aura.

Let light. She lights each panel. Fires twisting.

Whatever must seek out its partner and annihilate with it. A great love.

The expansion today is just a gas station. It is not spectacular carnage.

So one has a set of events from which one finds one can't escape

to reach a distant observer.   And a star is born.

Red giant, super giant, white dwarf.

We observe a large number of these white dwarf stars.

Giant Sirius, the brightest in the night sky,

dog star. What we could have been had not the star

been so present, too much presence

seeping out of us—red the I Love Lucy kerchief draped over the lamp.

A she-ness to the table.   Pearls on the bread plate, make-up on the
  napkin,

a couple of burned-out butts.

(Alien intake valves?)

And come night: a supper club.

High risk behavior in cinemascopic rain.

The heat released in this reaction,

which is like, a controlled hydrogen bomb explosion,

which is like, what makes stars shine.

Boy Pegasus   Boy Murcury   Sister Venus

the stars so compulsively readable   the sun eight light minutes away,

Birthmark. At the red end of the spectrum.

Three gold-jacketed overly friendly men smiling,

poling before the nymph of a red river   burning in the presence of the floor
  plans.

For the world is one world now   not that you may own your own home.

Sinter me, sister.   Threescore skullduggery,   endless cradle holding a space
  open.

Rufous skylark,   tell us off the skiff,

sun up, the next day,   we're looking into a box.

Let's see the world.   Are you coming with me.   What's for dinner.

1999

Robert Hass

Robert Hass was born in 1941 in San Francisco, California. In 1971, he earned his PhD from Stanford University. He is one of the most recognized and celebrated poets in America. The author of four books of poetry, *Field Guide, Praise, Human Wishes,* and *Sun Under Wood,* Hass has also written an award-winning book of criticism, *Twentieth Century Pleasures,* and collaborated with Nobel Laureate Czeslaw Milosz in translating Milosz's work from Polish. Further, he has translated a substantial body of haiku from the Japanese, edited *The Best American Poetry for 2001,* and, perhaps most notably, served as Poet Laureate of the United States from 1995-1997. Difficult to categorize, Hass combines an exceptional intelligence with an informal ease to create poetry that is memorable and challenging.

ENVY OF OTHER PEOPLE'S POEMS

In one version of the legend the sirens couldn't sing.
It was only a sailor's story that they could.
So Odysseus, lashed to the mast, was harrowed
By a music that he didn't hear—plungings of sea,
Wind-sheer, the off-shore hunger of the birds—
And the mute women gathering kelp for garden mulch,
Seeing him strain against the cordage, seeing
The awful longing in his eyes, are changed forever
On their rocky waste of island by their imagination
Of his imagination of the song they didn't sing.

1998-2004

A Supple Wreath of Myrtle

Poor Nietzsche in Turin, eating sausage his mother
Mails to him from Basel. A rented room,
A small square window framing August clouds
Above the mountain. Brooding on the form
Of things: the dangling spur
Of an Alpine columbine, winter-tortured trunks
Of cedar in the summer sun, the warp in the aspen's trunk
Where it torqued up through the snowpack.

"Every where the wasteland grows; woe
To him whose wasteland is within."

Dying of syphilis. Trimming a luxuriant mustache.
In love with the opera of Bizet.

1998–2004

FUTURES IN LILACS

"Tender little Buddha,"
She said of my least Buddha-like member.
She was probably quoting Allen Ginsberg,
Who was probably paraphrasing Walt Whitman.
After the Civil War, after the death of Lincoln,
That was a good time to own railroad stocks,
But he was in the Library of Congress
Researching alternative Americas,
Reading up on the curiosities of Hindoo philosophy,
Studying the etchings of stone carvings
Of strange couplings in a book.

She was taking off a blouse,
Almost transparent, the color of a silky tangerine.
From Capitol Hill Walt Whitman must have been able to see
Willows gathering the river haze
In the cooling and still-humid twilight.
He was in love with a trolley conductor

In the summer of—what was it?—1867? 1868?

1998-2004

The World as Will and Representation

When I was a child my father every morning—
Some mornings, for a time, when I was ten or so,
My father gave my mother a drug called antabuse.
It makes you sick if you drink alcohol.
There were little yellow pills. He ground them
In a glass, dissolved them in water, handed her
The glass and watched her closely while she drank.
It was the late nineteen-forties, a time,
A social world, in which the men got up
And went to work, leaving the women with the children.
His wink at me was a nineteen-forties wink.
He watched her closely so she couldn't "pull
A fast one" or "put anything over" on a pair
As shrewd as the two of us. I hear those phrases
In old movies and my mind begins to drift.
The reason he ground the medications fine
Was that the pills could be hidden under the tongue
And spit out later. The reason that this ritual
Occurred so early in the morning—I was told,
And knew it to be true—was that she could
If she wanted, induce herself to vomit,
So she had to be watched until her system had
Absorbed the drug. Hard to render, in these lines,
The rhythm of the act. He ground two of them
To powder in a glass, filled it with water,
Handed it to her, and watched her drink.
In my memory, he's wearing a suit, grey,
Herringbone, a white shirt she had ironed.
Some mornings, as in the comics we read
When Dagwood went off early to placate
Mr. Dithers, leaving Blondie with crusts
Of toast and yellow rivulets of egg yolk
To be cleared before she went shopping—
On what the comic called a shopping spree—
With Trixie, the next door neighbor, my father

Would catch an early bus and leave the task
Of vigilance to me. "Keep an eye on Mama, pardner."
You know the passage in the Aeneid? The man
Who leaves the burning city with his father
On his shoulders, holding his young son's hand,
Means to do well among the flaming arras
And the falling columns while the blind prophet,
Arms upraised, howls from the inner chamber,
"Great Troy is fallen. Great Troy is no more."
Slumped in a bathrobe, penitent and biddable,
My mother at the kitchen table gagged and drank,
Drank and gagged. We get our first moral idea
About the world—about justice and power,
Gender and the order of things—from somewhere.

1998-2004

TIME AND MATERIALS

Gerhard Richter: Abstrakt Bilden

1.

To make layers,
As if they were a steadiness of days:

It snowed; I did errands at a desk;
A white flurry out the window thickening; my tongue
Tasted of the glue on envelopes.

On this day sunlight on red brick, bare trees,
Nothing stirring in the icy air.

On this day a blur of color moving at the gym
Where the heat from bodies
Meets the watery, cold surface of the glass.

Made love, made curry, talked on the phone
To friends, the one whose brother died
Was crying and thinking alternately,
Like someone falling down and getting up
And running and falling and getting up.

2.

The object of this poem is not to annihila

To not annih

The object of this poem is to report a theft,
    In progress, of everything
That is not these words
    And their disposition on the page.

The object o   f this poem is to report a theft,
    In progre   ss of everything that exists
That is not th   ese words
    And their d   isposition on the page.

The object of his poe is t epro a theft
    In rogres f ever hing   at xists
Th   is no   ese w rds
    And their disp sit on o   the pag

   3.

To score, to scar, to smear, to streak,
To smudge, to blur, to gouge, to scrape.

'Action painting,' i.e.,
The painter gets to behave like time.

   4.

The typo wound be 'paining.'

(To abrade.)

   5.

Or to render time and stand outside
The horizontal rush of it, for a moment
To have the sensation of standing outside
The greenish rush of it.

   6.

Some vertical gesture then, the way that anger
Or desire can rip a life apart,

Some wound of color.

1998-2004

Brenda Hillman

Brenda Hillman was born in 1951 in Tucson, Arizona. A graduate of the Iowa Writers workshop, she has been associated both with the most experimental work coming out of the San Francisco Bay area and a more traditional lyric strain in American literature. Although she is profoundly interested in Gnosticism, she is also a poet very much involved with the mundanity of contemporary life; that is, her work does not shirk an attachment to the material world in its plummeting of gnosis. Her methods for uncovering the "secret knowledge"—mystical apprehension of the godhead—are as varied as the subject matter and formal shapes of her poetry. Hypnosis, radical textual experiments, even an attempt to render the transformative processes of alchemy in a textual representation on the page have all been elements of her practice. Brenda Hillman's six books of poetry—including *Bright Existence, Death Tractates, Loose Sugar,* and, most recently, *Cascadia*—constitute an important exploration of poetics and the spirit, an exploration compelled by aesthetic, political, and spiritual obsessions. She has received many awards for her poetry, including National Endowment for the Arts and Guggenheim fellowships.

ADULT JOY

The slender vessel used for weddings
was also used for funerals.
Loutrophoros. Handles curled
like rams' horns, and beneath some rigid frills,
the ghost-bride greets the master
of the underworld. Are terra-cotta
slaves running around with stylized
gestures on the back of the vase?
Nothing is obvious but that the bride
is confused. What was to be joy
is not continuing. Jagged
lightning designs. Death
greets her like a senator.
I sat last night in a cheap café
leaning on the dignity of a small table.
Worn carpet with an eighteenth century
pattern. And all around the room,
bent over silver paperbacks, eating
and being filled, others
like myself, one writing a treatise
on a napkin...How
did this sudden joy come in?
Joy by subtraction,
joy in the dim human realm...
I thought of Wordsworth's
formal joy fading in fourteen
lines commending him to death
or Herbert's childlike adjunct
to renunciation...No, it was
the little adult joy
he'd raised in me, pure, like the tube
of space-time after an accident:
the worst has already happened!
I flattened the book; the plate
of splendid vegetables arrived,

healthy food for the readers
of Berkeley whose faces glow
but not perfectly...The owner
slouched behind the counter,
selling his jars of night.
And under a grate on Center,
an iron ladder greeted the revised hell
where the pool shimmered, filled
the space that would transform
the wedding. The death-
bride adjusts her tiara ...Freud
walks to the desk; his favorite
statue, bronze Athena,
has lost her spear. We grow up.
Joy becomes the missing event,
what reaches us unknown
without wisdom. Joy is the spear.

1993

CHEAP GAS

That dithyramb of ticky-tick, boom,
brrrrr we hear when we lift
the nozzle, pull back on the black rubber
and shove it in—

the noise hums to a bigger rumble,
practically shakes the self-serve pump;
probably it's the ancient forests
growing higher, reversing the Pleistocene—
they're refusing to become Techroline Super-Unleaded,
the trees have decided not to leave their bodies
in the rotting executive swamps.

Blackened thumbs hold the credit card slips
in the clipboard, the sweet young
men tear off "customer copy,"
look us in the eye. Their names in wilted
red letters over their hearts:
Jake, Carlos, Todd with two d's. We should
read the names carefully through fumes
rising from rainbows of spilled gas on the station floor,
still pretty cheap. Full tank 13.69.

Removing the nozzle we should notice,
when the vagrant drop falls down, the liquid is still
pretty golden, pink dominates for an instant,
then forgets.
Doesn't look like the blood of young men,
liquid from bodies: tears, semen, blood, urine,
acids, the yellow drop
of cheap gas has all those in it. Bodies lie
in the sand and the ancient forests feel them over
and over and stop growing.

The Hanging Gardens of Nebuchadnezzar had one
of each kind of flower. We didn't bomb those.
The cruel king walked there with his personal servants;

we are his now.
we are tending the waters of cheap gas
where they fall. By the waters, slaves
lived for generations. By the waters
of Babylon they moved and spoke—

1997

The Unbeginning

—or, maybe you could just
give up on beginnings. After all,

this notion that things start
and end somewhere
has caused you so much trouble!

Look at the wild radish in the fields out there.
Isn't it always row
and row of pastel pink-
yellow-blue like some bargain
print of itself, in new pillowcases, on sale;

and you stumble
through it thinking art must come
from the book of splendor
or the book of longing
until the rhythms curve

and the previous music
hasn't ended yet:

the whir the blackbirds make,
as they land, sounds like velcro,
like a child undoing
velcro from the winter jacket

(from the *hood*
of the winter jacket)

1998

SHARED CUSTODY

An example often used to show ?? is *x* falling feet first into a singularity with a
watch on. Fate is what happens backwards. With regard to Persephone,
the seasons don't change till something agrees to her sacrifice.

When a child is dropped off in front of the other parent's house she creates a
history of space and yellow hurrying in the unopposed direction as we
learn to read by hurrying meaning.

She got out of the car. Smell-threads of Johnson's baby shampoo. Redolence exists
by itself as opportunity. The end of the Cold War had come. In Russia,
more oranges, lizard baskets of capitalism. I tried to talk to her father; he
tried to talk to me.

As *x* falls by prearrangement with the experimenters, yellow is unopposed. The
child, leaving the car, drops an alphabet on the path. y. e. l. Shaving of
yellow, central plaid, black from a fraction if she has been brave about
including the math.

She hated her little bag. A Thursday humming followed. My writing was falling
apart. She was learning to read.

A fate begins to be assembled when the linear is shared. All it does doesn't work.
Should dirt not praise her efforts? Little pointed

arrows swerve around the (from the mother's perspective) vanishing skirt. Flashes
of letters here. Here. Home is the fear of size. A word can fall apart. y. e.
We sat in the car. Tiny bats between Berkeley double-you'd the air.

The lip of singularity is an event too far beyond, good corduroy with its highs
and lows as the star dissolves in the just-having-spun and you're not
supposed to ask how *x* feels as he falls in. Persephone practices her yes,
her no, her this that and the other, the child approaching the house of the
father in motion of minutes, free for twenty yards of both of them, makes
a roof with her good-by : // bye \\ mom. They'll have to invent new
seasons to explain it.

A daughter grows a horizon. Somehow a line by which a life could be pursued.

When she started to read, I no longer heard language, it heard me. I had the stupid
idea that she should dress up to leave.

x should have checked with Persephone about the kicking and screaming. I should
have checked with the mother but I was the mother. Backward should try
to fix loss so it is not devastation but chronicle.

Panic plaid, almost at his door, *I cannot see what flowers are.* Daffodils. Dirt's
birthday candles. California is medium old. *x* won't be very young when
he gets to the center, nor will the child, testifying to the cloth, dropped, sent
back fractal, active as the buoys on the bay, nor is the child very young.

If you are time you think in terms of next. If you are Persephone you think in
terms of dirt. If you're the metaphor you'll let the thing stand for it. On
Monday the flash of a dove, your hoping

frame. The child *can* look back, the myths don't apply here, if you think one joy
was sacrificed it's because you said it. What choice did it have when the
thing undid but to call her in broken colors.

2001

Pre-Uplift of the Sierra

Hermit thrush ,??;;&~ (having chosen the wrong female)—

(Queen Lear,
sometimes sometimes
sometimes sometimes sometimes)—;

had stopped
having respect for time, not for color or substance.

Cher taking it back about being sorry she's fifty.

Eight blues at Meeks Bay not counting the four skies;

others tried to *be* so they stuck to one thing;   sorry, not today.

The faultline is god's palm being read under the sand
where the families are lying:

heartline~   head—

an obsession helpless in the face of ecstasy.

It was August   glacial debris   pieces

of a life reminiscing about the pre-uplift:

outcrops of mudstones and shales,

harmony;

a woman washed her black hat in the lake:

"Anytime you mainstream a hat to the family
there's always a risk."

What is the half-life of having one?

I was half-listening to infinity
when we spoke.

Every sentence was the skin of heaven.

2001

Edward Hirsch

Edward Hirsch was born in Chicago, Illinois, in 1950. He was educated at Grinnell College and the University of Pennsylvania, where he earned his doctorate. Hirsch has taught at several colleges and universities, and presently serves as the president of the Guggenheim Foundation. A poet of diverse talents—utilizing narrative, lyrical, and dramatic elements—his books of poetry include *For the Sleepwalkers, Wild Gratitude, The Night Parade, Earthly Measures, Lay Back the Darkness*, and, most recently, *On Love*. He has also written *How to Read a Poem and Fall in Love with Poetry*, a book on the appreciation of poetry. He has won many awards, including a Guggenheim Fellowship, the National Book Critics Circle Award, and a MacArthur Fellowship.

And So It Begins Again

This morning it is
The sky hanging behind the river
Like a mottled sheet, a coarse
Blue shirt spangled with pears.
It is the obvious crescent of my own face
Fading on the glass, the steam

From my mouth, steam
From a slow tugboat tugged slowly
Through the iron petals of a bridge
Opening and, yes, clanging shut. It is
A nameless wound swelling under my tongue,
The soft wings beating in my chest, and
The last pigeons breaking out of the water
Like a flurry of snowflakes and fists.

On the other side of the bridge
There is a boy banking a small fire
Of twigs, warming his hands on the flame,
And watching a thin vein of smoke
Merging with a light mist from the river,
A crescent of steam, and a final patch of moon
Faltering in a thicket of chimneys. He has
So many thoughts, so many other secrets
Entangled in that artery of smoke
Scrawled across the wind like a signature.

And so it begins again
Here and now, like this, in our world.
Because it *is* our world, because
The veils are lifting from our windows
And the other faces appear, looking out
At our life together, our new day starting up
With the light from a small fire
Rising into a sky of fists and stars.

1976

THE CHARDIN EXHIBITION

(for William Maxwell, 1908-2000)

While I was studying the copper cistern
and the silver goblet, a soup tureen
with a cat stalking a partridge and hare,

you were gulping down the morning light
and moving from the bedstand to the bureau,
from the shuttered window to the open door.

While I was taking my time over a pristine jar
of apricots and a basket of wild strawberries—
a pyramid leaning toward a faceted glass—

you were sitting at a low breakfast table
and eating a soft-boiled egg—just one—
from a tiny, hesitant, glittering spoon.

While I was absorbed in a duck hanging
by one leg and a hare with a powder flask
and a game bag, which you wanted me to see,

you were lying on the living-room couch
for a nap, one of your last, next to
a white porcelain vase with two carnations.

I wish I could have stood there with you
in front of Chardin's last self-portrait,
exclaiming over his turban with a bow

and the red splash of his pastel crayon—
a new medium—which he used, dearest,
to defy death on a sheet of blue paper.

2002

SELF-PORTRAIT

I lived between my heart and my head,
like a married couple who can't get along.

I lived between my left arm, which is swift
and sinister, and my right, which is righteous.

I lived between a laugh and a scowl,
and voted against myself, a two-party system.

My left leg dawdled or danced along,
my right cleaved to the straight and narrow.

My left shoulder was like a stripper on vacation,
my right stood upright as a Roman soldier.

Let's just say that my left side was the organ
donor and leave my private parts alone,

but as for my eyes, which are two shades
of brown, well, Dionysus meet Apollo.

Look at Eve raising her left eyebrow
while Adam puts his right foot down.

No one expected it to survive,
but divorce seemed out of the question.

I suppose my left hand and my right hand
will be clasped over my chest in the coffin

and I'll be reconciled at last,
I'll be whole again

2004

Boy with a Headset

He is wearing baggy shorts and a loud T-shirt
and singing along to his headset on Broadway.
Every now and then he glances back at me,
a middle-aged father weaving through traffic behind him.

He is a 15-year-old in the city—no more, no less—
but I imagine him as a colorful unnamed bird
warbling his difference from the robins and sparrows
and scissoring past the vendors on every corner.

I keep thinking of him as a wild fledgling
who tilts precariously on one wing
and peers back at me from the sudden height
before sailing out over the treetops.

2004

The History of My Stupidity: Volume 3, Chapter 5

The history of my stupidity would fill many volumes.

—*Czeslaw Milosz*

Traffic was heavy coming off the bridge
and I took the road to the right, the wrong one,
and got stuck in the car for hours.

Most nights I rushed out into the evening
without paying attention to the trees,
whose names I didn't know,
or the birds, who flew heedlessly on.

I couldn't relinquish my desires
or accept them, and so I strolled along
like a tiger who wanted to spring,
but was still afraid of the wildness within.

The iron bars seemed invisible to others,
but I carried a cage around inside me.

I cared too much what other people thought
and made remarks I shouldn't have made.
I was silent when I should have spoken.

Forgive me, philosophers,
I read the Stoics but never understood them.

I felt that I was living the wrong life,
spiritually speaking,
while half way around the world
thousands of people were being slaughtered,
some of them by my countrymen.

So I walked on—distracted, lost in thought—
and forgot to attend to those who suffered
far away, nearby.

Forgive me, faith, for never having any.

I did not believe in God,
who eluded me.

2004

Christopher Howell

Christopher Howell was born in Portland, Oregon, in 1945. The author of eight books of poetry, including *Sweet Afton, The Crime of Luck, Sea Change, Memory and Heaven,* and *Light's Ladder,* Christopher Howell has been praised by writers ranging from James Tate to William Tremblay. That range of praise speaks to the variety of quality work Howell has produced—as well as the uniqueness of his vision. Lyrical and narrative threads, sharp declaration and musing meditation, clear imagery and surreal atmosphere, incisive monologues and dreamy visions: Howell's poetry draws on a variety of traditions and practices. Editor of the successful, independent Lynx House Press, he lives in Spokane, Washington, where he teaches in the MFA program at Eastern Washington University.

IN THE SPRING OF HJALMAR CALRSON: THE REAL STORY

I saw you there, at the end
Of Karl Johan Gate
Where the Palace Gardens swoop
Down to the city
Like a wedge of green birds.
I knew you would stop, puzzled
And pleased to ask after the ship
Which had borne me there,
That you would lead me home
And up those four stacks
Of wooden stairs. And the one
Room was the room I knew
Would greet me, simply
The pad on the floor bathed
In a butter of late northern light,
The one chair against the desk
Of books and candles. The tapestry.
But I did not foresee
Desire, as you said quietly I could
Allow this, I could
Love here once in this dazzled
Air. But it would not be
The truth. The truth, that ship,
Is bound far from these hours
And the days of longing
Will be like a mountain's longing
For the sky. But your hand
Against the wet swaying grass
Of me, its stillness: loss
For the sake of memory.
So we stayed
As I could not have known
We would, in bright midnight, hands

Surrendering their urgency, voices
Calmly playing the endless
Only night we knew.

1991

THE BRIDE OF LONG DIVISION

Water spiders dissemble the light and spillage
of day
and my ribbons and portraits agree
that if what goes around comes around
like whips of the angels, I must be
divided just to live
as rivers live
with the moving sticks and leaves and tumbling
stones. Just to live I must have the bride
who wears me like shoes
taking their separate ignorant steps
toward the water spider's palace of edges and seams.
If I love her, how will I know it
from love of myself? If she makes for me
a perfect tabulation of the indivisible
which it is thought only the beasts achieve,
how will I bear the duplicity of touching
her again? How can the shadow
go on without the self to dance with
across the tense surface of mind
while something else looks up with adoration
from a deeper place and something else
comes home to reeds and lilies, groom and last remainder,
describing it all?

1996

THE CHRISTIAN SCIENCE MINOTAUR

He is half bull
and half book
and he eats broccoli, mostly,
with sauce. He says, "I wish
I could kill something
or smoke."
But his room is only open
10 to 4 and nothing is allowed
in but eyeglasses and the curious
who stare straight at him and yawn.
When nights get bad
and he has again read through
himself without solving the riddle
of a life without hospitals
or booze, he lifts the Venetian blinds
and broods out through the gold-leaf lettering,
and thinks, "Surely they will send youths
or a clever boy with string."
And surely they do not send him anything
but the thin, impalpable subscriptions
no good to eat. And he *is* hungry,
though his soul, it is said, is stuffed
with all that's good for him.

1996

HE WRITES TO THE SOUL

I'm just jotting this note so you won't forget
that though life is blue behind me and stony
in the instants I pause for, I have beads and shells
enough to hold back a sidelong toppling. Anyway,
at every crossing I kneel and say "excelsior"
and light a little fire in a jar and drink it down,
hoping if fire's a prayer no one will answer it just yet.
But I guess that's clear. At first I thought I'd write you
about the hemp-trap roses that grow by collapsing
and bringing home whatever's trying to sniff them
at the time, about what that means. Then I thought
that's just peering at the innards of luck, and no good
comes of such haruspicy. So I guess I'll give you
news about the lake dark which is growing, too,
and just yesterday began working up into the sky
among softball and badminton of the angels.
Lucky they were already wearing headlamps
to bedazzle the fish up there! Lucky their suede rings
keep their hands afloat, otherwise who knows
how they'd copy down the Braille God keeps sending
like flocks of perforated swans? Some good news is
the apple tornadoes are out of blossom now
and have become zinc, which as you know
says very little and requires practically no disaster.
That's what Mom says, anyway, and she should know.
She says she knows about you, too. She says
you are the shade of something folded and alone
on a long leash of red pearls and that God
put you there because he couldn't help it.
But I don't know, I think you're somehow related
to this lake…like its language maybe, or like the idea
of swimming, which I've always enjoyed. Well, that's it,
I guess. Don't fret about my safety; if the weather
doesn't suck its trigger finger while it hunts for time,
or if something huge and golden lets me have its keys,

I'll be OK. Lake or no lake, some days I feel
perfectly disguised in front of you, like intention
around an iceberg or sunlight on the skin of the rain.
And I'm happy now, happy as a jungle, happy as a wisp
of dreaming melon and I cry only on your days off.

2003

THE NEW ORPHEUS

For Emma (1981-2001)

As though all windows had been nailed shut
I look out at the blank insides
of my eyes. Who lives here
in fire so deep it loves the water?
A handful of shells and a peacock moon
lie down in the dark of my arm.
Pins and needles, sorrow and salt: I'm trying
hard to match things up
with their Platonic other shinings.
I need more time for this
place I need to open like a door of rain,
like everthing coming down
because of blue saturations of the unforgettable
and too unbearable to know.
I'm giving myself just one
more lifetime of prying and pulling
at my hinges, beating the old empty roses
my daughter walks in, thinking I've been away
too long now, it's getting late, they're slamming
the other world and dousing the lights.
Rain and rain again, old winter. It's really dark
where she is. All night I lie awake, building a ladder
of light.

2003

Claudia Keelan

Claudia Keelan was born in 1959 in Anaheim, California. She has published five books of poetry, including *Refinery*, *The Secularist*, *Utopic*, and *The Devotion Field*. Keelan's poetry is concerned with justice amid the damaging dynamics of a frequently hurtful culture. Positing a necessary change in perspective from the rigorous hierarchies and categories of a violent world, Keelan's poems seek a method to articulate her embrace of the provisional and indeterminate. Through the articulation of shifting methods, Keelan hopes to bring readers to an acceptance of indeterminacy as a way to compassion. A graduate of the University of Iowa Writers' Workshop, Keelan directs the MFA International Program at the University of Nevada, Las Vegas.

Romanticism

It is not the clay road
on which a woman travels
clutching a baby in one arm
and holding an older boy's hand
while he eats an apple.
I think it must be
in what the boy sees as he walks
there, caught in the sweetness
of apple, in the love it allows
him as he bites suddenly
his cheek, as he turns his face
up to his mother, wanting to cry
but stopping himself, *how tired
she is* and he has only just begun
to bleed. And it's how I want
to let him keep looking away
from her who has his hand,
at wild flowers, the old town,
anywhere but at his feet.

1994

The End is an Animal

The hole the day digs for your feeling is opening now. Let it go.
Let it go or follow it in, kicking over the precipice—what does it
    matter?
It's not yours anymore. Puddles deepen in this sudden thaw, a
    hand
lifting—do you feel it?—from your mouth, breath stabilizing,
    you call *this*
the spirit of matter? Nothing huge and old and incredibly
    wise is living
under the field somewhere. And what drifts against your throat
    sometimes—oh pity
it. Muttering weak God, patron of aneurysm, production lines,
    patron
of food banks and cool water, dear intelligence!

    Dear Gnosis, most holy note: For weeks now, driving in my car,
attempts to *know* the story pouring from the announcer's mouth,
    I've felt
your bruised will sobbing from the periphery of the road. I swear
it was your soundless agony hurling from the tree line, to the
    houses'
small lights, and back. You passed through the car and I couldn't
touch you. Teacher, the body of God is a mass grave. In him
the souls are reeling and he is rocking them now in the grass and
    calling
us by name. Under the shifting clouds, he is rocking and calling
our names.

    In the hole, birds thread straw through the eyes or your feeling.
She is the loneliest of girls, having forgiven even your
    abandonment.

She is the body keeping you from yourself, from God. She cringes at your interrogations, she is flesh lampshade, she is a million ID tags, she is the sensation inside your bones. She is all that is true, beautiful girl, taken into a coma by one after the other, into death and still they won't leave her. And when you mumble *why God*, it is her face, not his, that kisses your lids to sleep. Hear her whisper *it's not his fault.*

1997

THE SECULARIST

I. Grammar of Assent

So the world became me

and I became blind

$$\text{(as I wished)}$$

light itself shrinking

into a word that spread

a long shadow across the Bureaus

where I signed my name.

Days and days of tangible bread,

functional shoes. Afternoons,

I teach them my language:

Bread, cup, tool.

They want more,

love for example,

and *travel*, wind in grass

of fields I no longer see.

Evenings, the last light

no longer insistent

in the oil ponds and leaves.

An overhead bulb caressing my set of dictionaries.

Even in the machine

there should be equality.

No part subordinate

to any other part

though in function and process

one body, one part

must of necessity be

subordinate to another.

But the desire for chaos had arisen:

all should be equal,

the subway's rotarian industry

canceling destination in each

stop of the train, the dull

exclamations of steeple and factory

punctuating as far as I could see.

Why should my heart be the piece

I can't form correctly

On the flypress? I keep trying,

Losing whole days of wages.

Blind or not, the light's warmth

or lack thereof

finds me at the wheel.

Power failure.

Didn't make the rate.

In the utmost logic of exile,

All aims waste toward an elsewhere.

Didn't make the rate.

You know how much I used to like Plato.

Today I realized he lied.

This world is not a reflection of the ideal,

But of we who are filthy and die.

The tool forms them and makes a hole.

Not belonging to any place, any time, any love.

2. Apology

My son, my only,

fed now and asleep,
exile stiffens into presence

on the periphery

of the graveyard and headstone's seller's

functional, corner lot.

It was Christ

-mas, rows of wreaths

punctuated the graves, rows

and rows of consolation

and habit in evergreen

and red ribbon. Oh elsewhere,

I could not go in. Couldn't pass

the gate prohibiting dogs and bicycles,

couldn't stride past the seraphim,

in. Standing by the ridiculous markers,

my breasts leaking milk, wanting to buy

one. Plain gray. No name, no years,

wanting to plant the stone and have it finished.

In the end, I couldn't love

the others nor the balloons

someone dared among the wreaths

but turned back toward

the God's dead son in the middle

of the cemetery, his mute suffering

word of my word, flesh of my—

I do not lend my ashes

to this ground.

The smoke rising above the city

has absolutely nothing to forgive.

1997

EMBERS

Apologize for birth &
         convey more being.
What is true outside
is equally true inside.
Apologize and convey.
Believe unprovoked suffering
         speaks unrivaled,
silent suffering
         speaks unrivaled.
It is solid work   it is always true.

2000

My Twentieth Century

It is better   to appear
        untrue   than to be   untrue:
        their prayers   a mechanical intonation of a bird.

I   is not a writer
                            to serve the cause of language.
The language I knows
                            commits errors knowingly,
prayer's language   a tool: a cow put to the knife.

The remedy lies in readers,   "Summit Dwellers,"   English,
                            despite I's and Our's
                            best efforts.

Remedy   commits
errors knowingly,
in English,   imitation without
                                        domination,
Mother-tongue   without imitation:
        "the bowels of the earth"
        "the womb of the earth"
                            very sweet
                            without domination.
Expression   innocent fun.

Whether construction is permissible or not
prayer/a bird/I on behalf of readers
invite "summit dwellers" say

It is better to appear to
than to be to

2000

Yusef Komunyakaa

Yusef Komunyakaa was born in 1947 in Bogalusa, Louisiana. He received an MA from Colorado State University and an MFA in creative writing from the University of California, Irvine, in 1980. Komunyakaa's poetry has been celebrated by many distinctions, including a Kingsley Tufts Award, the Ruth Lilly Prize, and his nomination to the American Academy of Poets. From what many view as his breakthrough book, *Copacetic*, to his recently published *Talking Dirty to the Gods* and *Taboo : The Wishbone Trilogy, Part 1*, Komunyakaa's experiences in Vietnam and as an African American growing up in the south combined with a fervent attraction to jazz and blues have led to the shaping of an important body of work. Other books of Komunyakaa's include *Lost in the Bonewheel Factory, Neon Vernacular*, for which he won the Pulitzer Prize, *Dien Cai Dau*, and *Thieves of Paradise*. He is currently a professor of creative writing at Princeton University.

URBAN RENEWAL

The sun slides down behind brick dust,
today's angle of life. Everything

melts, even when backbones
are I-beams braced for impact.

Sequential sledgehammers fall, stone
shaped into dry air

white sound system of loose metal
under every footstep. Wrecking crews,

men unable to catch sparrows without breaking
wings into splinters. Blues-horn

mercy. Bloodlines. Nothing
but the white odor of absence.

The big iron ball
swings, keeping time

to pigeons cooing in eaves
as black feathers

float on to blueprint
parking lots.

1977

LET'S SAY

He leans over—well,
let's say his name's Nilo
& he's black in Argentina.
He bends to look into his eyes
staring back *nada*
from a starry limbo,
balancing his world
on an eyelash.

Down there chance
distills into booze
& he sees himself walking
on the sea floor.
The small miserable boat
bobs over his head.

By midday someone
has already taken over
his stall in the marketplace
where the village opens
into a tango, every red-sash day.

The new man, Vazquez,
who has a lover & a wife
five miles down the road,
drags in his display
of sea bass, squid,
black eel, blood trail,
singing *"Para Nosotros"*
under his white breath.

1984

AMBUSH

So quiet birds
start singing again.
Lizards bring a touch of light.
The squad leader counts bullets
a third time. Stars
glint off gunbarrels.
We can almost hear a leaf
falling. "For chrissake. Please."
Raw opium intoxicates
a blaze of insects.
Buddhist monks on a hill
burn twelve red lanterns.
"Put out your stupid cigarette,
PFC," the Recon corporal whispers.
The trees play games.
A tiger circles us, in his broken cage
between the sky & what's human.
"We'll wait out the bastards.
They have to come this way,
& when they do, not
even God can help 'em."
Headless shadows skirt the hedgerow.
A crossroad for lost birds
calling to the dead,
& then a sound that makes you jump
in your sleep years later,
the cough of a mortar tube.

1986

STARLIGHT SCOPE MYOPIA

Gray-blue shadows lift
shadows onto an oxcart.

Making night work for us,
the starlight scope brings
men into killing range.

The river under Vi Bridge
takes the heart away

like the Water God
riding his dragon.
Smoke-colored

Viet Cong
move under our eyelids,

lords over loneliness
winding like coral vine through
sandalwood & lotus,

inside our lowered heads
years after this scene

ends. The brain closes
down. What looks like
one step into the trees,

they're lifting crates of ammo
& sacks of rice, swaying

under their shared weight.
Caught in the infrared,
what are they saying?

Are they talking about women
or calling the Americans

beaucoup dien cai dau?
One of them is laughing.
You want to place a finger

to his lips & say "shhhh."
You try reading ghost talk

on their lips. They say
"up-up we go," lifting as one.
This one, old, bowlegged,

you feel you could reach out
& take him into your arms. You

peer down the sights of your M-16,
seeing the full moon
loaded on an oxcart.

1988

ONCE THE DREAM BEGINS

I wish the bell saved you.
  "Float like a butterfly
& sting like a bee."

Too bad you didn't
  learn to disappear
before a left jab.

Fighting your way out of a clench,
  you counter-punched & bicycled
but it was already too late—

gray weather had started
  shoving the sun into a corner.
"He didn't mess up my face."

But he was an iron hammer
  against stone, as you
bobbed & weaved through hooks.

Now we strain to hear you.
  Once the dream begins
to erase itself, can the

dissolve be stopped?
  No more card tricks
for the TV cameras,

Ali. Please come back to us
  sharp-tongued & quick-footed,
spinning out of the blurred

dance. Whoever said men
hit harder when women
are around, is right.

Word for word,
we beat the love
out of each other.

2001

Dorianne Laux

Born in 1952 in Augusta, Maine, Dorianne Laux's route to poetry has been different than that of many other contemporary poets; a single mother who held down jobs as gas station attendant, sanitarium cook, and maid—among others—before emerging as a poet, her work is charged with a grittiness that makes it memorable and compelling. Laux's first book of poems, _Awake_, was published in 1990; two subsequent volumes, _What We Carry_ and, most recently, _Smoke_, have continued to explore Laux's unique capacity to conflate lyricism with narrative strategies in poems littered with the everyday—from laundromats to Led Zeppelin, her work embraces and transforms everything it contains. The recipient of National Endowment for the Arts and Guggenheim Fellowships, Laux teaches in the creative writing program at the University of Oregon.

WHAT COULD HAPPEN

Noon. A stale Saturday. The hills
rise above the town, nudge houses and shops
toward the valley, kick the shallow river
into place. Here, a dog can bark for days

and no one will care enough
to toss an empty can or an unread newspaper
in his direction. No one complains.
The men stand in loose knots

outside Ace Hardware, talk a little, stare
at the blue tools. A few kids
sulk through the park, the sandbox full
of hardscrabble, the monkey bars

too hot to touch. In a town like this
a woman on the edge of forty
could drive around in her old car, the back end
all jingle and rivet, one headlight

taped in place, the hood held down with greasy rope,
and no one would notice.
She could drive up and down the same street
all day, eating persimmons,

stopping only for a moment to wonder
at the wooden Indian on the corner of 6th and B,
the shop window behind it
filled with beaten leather, bright woven goods

from Guatemala, postcards of this town
before it began to go under, began
to fade into a likeness of itself.
She could pull in at the corner store for a soda

and pause before uncapping it,
press the cold glass against her cheek,
roll it under her palm down the length of her neck
then slip it beneath the V of her blouse

and let it rest there, where she's hottest.
She could get back in her car
and turn the key, bring the engine up
like a swarm of bottle flies, feel it

shake like an empty caboose.
She could twist the radio too high
and drive like this for the rest of the day—
the same street, the same hairpin turn

that knocks the jack in the trunk from one wheel well
to the other—or she could pass the turn
and keep going, the cold soda
wedged between her legs, the bass notes

throbbing like a vein, out past the closed shops
and squat houses, the church
with its bland white arch, toward the hills,
beyond that shadowy nest of red madrones.

1994

FIRESTARTER

for my nephew, Raymond

Since this morning he's gone through
an entire box of Safeway matches, the ones
with the outlines of presidents' faces
printed in red, white and blue.
He's not satisfied with one match at a time.
He likes to tip the book over the ashtray
and light them all up at once, the flame
less than an inch from his fingertips
while the fathers of the nation burn.
He doesn't care about democracy,
or even anarchy, or the message inside
that promises art school for half price
if he'll complete the profile of a woman
and send it in. The street address burns,
ZIP code and phone number, the birth
and death dates of the presidents,
the woman's unfinished face. I'm afraid
he'll do this when I'm not around to keep him
from torching the curtains, the couch.
He strikes match after match, a small pyre rising
from the kitchen table. I ought to tell him
about Prometheus and the vulture, the wildfires
burning in the Oregon hills.
I want to do what I should do
and make him afraid, but his face
is radiant, ablaze with power,
and I can't take my eyes from the light.

2000

SMOKE

Who would want to give it up, the coal
a cat's eye in the dark room, no one there
but you and your smoke, the window
cracked to street sounds, the distant cries
of living things. Alone, you are almost
safe, smoke slipping out between the sill
and the glass, sucked into the night
you don't dare enter, its eyes drunk
and swimming with stars. Somewhere
a Dumpster is ratcheted open by the claws
of a black machine. All down the block
something inside you opens and shuts.
Sinister screech, pneumatic wheeze,
trash slams into the chute: leftovers, empties.
You don't flip on the TV or the radio, they
might muffle the sound of car engines
backfiring, and in the silence between,
streetlights twitching from green to red, scoff
of footsteps, the rasp of breath, your own,
growing lighter and lighter as you inhale.
There's no music for this scarf of smoke
wrapped around your shoulders, its fingers
crawling the pale stem of your neck,
no song light enough, liquid enough,
that climbs high enough before it thins
and disappears. Death's shovel scrapes
the sidewalk, critches across the man-made
cracks, slides on grease into rain-filled gutters,
digs its beveled nose among the ravaged leaves.
You can hear him weaving his way
down the street, sloshed on the last breath
he swirled past his teeth before swallowing:
breath of the cat kicked to the curb, a woman's
sharp gasp, lung-filled wail of the shaken child.
You can't put it out, can't stamp out the light

and let the night enter you, let it burrow through
your infinite passages. So you listen and listen
and smoke and give thanks, suck deep
with the grace of the living, blowing halos
and nooses and zeros and rings, the blue chains
linking around your head. Then you pull it in
again, the vein-colored smoke,
and blow it up toward a ceiling you can't see
where it lingers like a sweetness you can never hold,
like the ghost the night will become.

2000

PRAYER

Sweet Jesus, let her save you, let her take
your hands and hold them to her breasts,
slip the sandals from your feet, lay your body down
on sheets beaten clean against the fountain stones.
Let her rest her dark head on your chest,
let her tongue lift the fine hairs like a sword tip
parting the reeds, let her lips burnish
your neck, let your eyes be wet with pleasure.
Let her keep you from that other life, as a mother
keeps a child from the brick lip of a well,
though the rope and bucket shine and clang,
though the water's hidden silk and mystery call.
Let her patter soothe you and her passions
distract you, let her show you the light
storming the windows of her kitchen, peaches
in a wooden bowl, a square of blue cloth
she has sewn to her skirt to cover the tear.
What could be more holy than the curve of her back
as she sits, her hands opening a plum.
What could be more sacred than her eyes,
fierce and complicated as the truth, your life
rising behind them, your name on her lips.
Stay there, in her bare house, the black pots
hung from pegs, bread braided and glazed
on the table, a clay jug of violet wine.
There is the daily sacrament of rasp and chisel,
another chair to be made, shelves to be hewn
cleanly and even and carefully joined
to the sun-scrubbed walls, a sharp knife
for carving odd chunks of wood into small toys
for the children. Oh Jesus, close your eyes

and listen to it, the air is alive with bird calls
and bees, the dry rustle of palm leaves,
her distracted song as she washes her feet.
Let your death be quiet and ordinary.
Either life you choose will end in her arms.

2000

Trying To Raise The Dead

Look at me. I'm standing on a deck
in the middle of Oregon. There are
friends inside the house. It's not my

house, you don't know them.
They're drinking and singing
and playing guitars. You love

this song, remember, "Ophelia,"
*Boards on the windows, mail
by the door.* I'm whispering

so they won't think I'm crazy.
They don't know me that well,
Where are you now? I feel stupid.

I'm talking to trees, to leaves
swarming on the black air, stars
blinking in and out of heart-

shaped shadows, to the moon, half-
lit and barren, stuck like an ax
between the branches. What are you

now? Air? Mist? Dust? Light?
What? Give me something. I have
to know where to send my voice.

A direction. An object. My love, it needs
a place to rest. Say anything. I'm listening.
I'm ready to believe. Even lies, I don't care.

Say *burning bush*. Say *stone*. They've
stopped singing now and I really should go.
So tell me, quickly. It's April. I'm

on Spring Street. That's my gray car
in the driveway. They're laughing
and dancing. Someone's bound

to show up soon. I'm waving.
Give me a sign if you can see me.
I'm the only one here on my knees.

2000

Li-Young Lee

Li-Young Lee was born in 1957 in Jakarta, Indonesia; after several years of wandering exile in Southeast Asia, his family moved to the United States. Driven by attention, passion, and lyricism, Li-Young Lee's poetry has received many awards and high praise from various critical perspectives. He has published three volumes of poetry, *Rose, The City in Which I Love You,* and *Book of my Nights*. Each of these books explores familial relationships, the enduring resonance of memory, and the self's search for the divine. His prose memoir, *The Winged Seed*, recounts his family's plight into exile and Lee's struggle to shape his past and present selves into a recognizable form of which he can make sense. Written in lyrical, sometimes surreal prose, the book probes the limits of language and reveals the tenuous hold we have both on memory and the immediate moment.

From Blossoms

From blossoms comes
this brown paper bag of peaches
we bought from the boy
at the bend in the road where we turned toward
signs painted *Peaches.*

From laden boughs, from hands,
from sweet fellowship in the bins,
comes nectar at the roadside, succulent
peaches we devour, dusty skin and all,
comes the familiar dust of summer, dust we eat.

O, to take what we love inside,
to carry within us an orchard, to eat
not only the skin, but the shade,
not only the sugar, but the days, to hold
the fruit in our hands, adore it, then bite into
the round jubilance of peach.

There are days we live
as if death were nowhere
in the background; from joy
to joy to joy, from wing to wing,
from blossom to blossom to
impossible blossom, to sweet impossible blossom.

1986

THE GIFT

To pull the metal splinter from my palm
my father recited a story in a low voice.
I watched his lovely face and not the blade.
Before the story ended, he'd removed
the iron silver I thought I'd die from.

I can't remember the tale,
but hear his voice still, a well
of dark water, a prayer.
And I recall his hands,
two measures of tenderness
he laid against my face,
the flames of discipline
he raised above my head.

Had you entered that afternoon
you would have thought you saw a man
planting something in a boy's palm,
a silver tear, a tiny flame.
Had you followed that boy
you would have arrived here,
where I bend over my wife's right hand.

Look how I shave her thumbnail down
so carefully she feels no pain.
Watch as I lift the splinter out.
I was seven when my father
took my hand like this,
and I did not hold that shard
between my fingers and think,
Metal that will bury me,
christen it Little Assassin,
Ore Going Deep for My Heart.
And I did not lift up my wound and cry,

Death visited here!
I did what a child does
when he's given something to keep.
I kissed my father.

1986

This Room and Everything In It

Lie still now
while I prepare for my future,
certain hard days ahead,
when I'll need what I know so clearly this moment.

I am making use
of the one thing I learned
of all the things my father tried to teach me:
the art of memory.

I am letting this room
and everything in it
stand for my ideas about love
and its difficulties.

I'll let your love-cries,
those spacious notes
of a moment ago,
stand for distance.

Your scent,
that scent
of spice and a wound,
I'll let stand for mystery.

Your sunken belly
is the daily cup
of milk I drank
as a boy before morning prayer.

The sun on the face
of the wall
is God, the face
I can't see, my soul,

and so on, each thing
standing for a separate idea,
and those ideas forming the constellation
of my greater idea.
And one day, when I need
to tell myself something intelligent
about love,

I'll close my eyes
and recall this room and everything in it:
My body is estrangement.
This desire, perfection.
Your closed eyes my extinction.
Now I've forgotten my
idea. The book
on the windowsill, riffled by wind...
the even-numbered pages are
the past, the odd-
numbered pages, the future.
The sun is
God, your body is milk...

useless, useless...
your cries are song, my body's not me...
no good...my idea
has evaporated...your hair is time, your thighs are song...
it had something to do
with death...it had something
to do with love.

1990

THE CLEAVING

He gossips like my grandmother, this man
with my face, and I could stand
amused all afternoon
in the Hon Kee Grocery,
amid hanging meats he
chops: roast pork cut
from a hog hung
by nose and shoulders,
her entire skin burnt
crisp, flesh I know
to be sweet,
her shining
face grinning
up at ducks
dangling single file,
each pierced by black
hooks through breast, bill,
and steaming from a hole
stitched shut at the ass.
I step to the counter, recite,
and he, without even slightly
varying the rhythm of his current confession or harangue,
scribbles my order on a greasy receipt,
and chops it up quick.

Such a sorrowful Chinese face,
nomad, Gobi, Northern
in its boniness
clear from the high
warlike forehead
to the sheer edge of the jaw.
He could by my brother, but finer,
and, except for his left forearm, which is engorged,
sinewy from his daily grip and
wield of a two-pound tool,

he's delicate, narrow-
waisted, his frame
so slight a lover, some
rough other
might break it down
its smooth, oily length.
In his light-handed calligraphy
on receipts and in his
moodiness, he is
a Southerner from a river-province;
suited for scholarship, his face poised
above an open book, he'd mumble
his favorite passages.
He could be my grandfather;
come to America to get a Western education
in 1917, but too homesick to study,
he sits in the park all day, reading poems
and writing letters to his mother.

He lops the head off, chops
the neck of the duck
into six, slits
the body
open, groin
to breast, and drains
the scalding juices,
then quarters the carcass
with two fast hacks of the cleaver,
old blade that has worn
into the surface of the round
foot-thick chop-block
a scoop that cradles precisely the curved steel.

The head, flung from the body, opens
down the middle where the butcher
cleanly halved it between
the eyes, and I

see, foetal-crouched
inside the skull, the homunculus,
gray brain grainy
to eat.
Did this animal, after all, at the moment
its neck broke,
image the way his executioner
shrinks from his own death?
Is this how
I, too, recoil from my day?
See how his shape
hordes itself, see how
little it is.
See its grease on the blade.
Is this how I'll be found
when judgment is passed, when names
are called, when crimes are tallied?
This is also how I looked before I tore my mother open.
Is this how I presided over my century, is this how
I regarded the murders?
This is also how I prayed.
Was it me in the Other
I prayed to when I prayed?
This too was how I slept, clutching my wife.
Was it me in the other I loved
when I loved another?
The butcher sees me eye this delicacy.
With a finger, he picks it
out of the skull-cradle
and offers it to me.
I take it gingerly between my fingers
and suck it down.
I eat my man.

The noise the body makes
when the body meets
the soul over the soul's ocean and penumbra

is the old sound of up-and-down, in-and-out,
a lump of muscle chug-chugging blood
into the ear; a lover's
heart-shaped tongue;
flesh rocking flesh until flesh comes;
the butcher working
at his block and blade to marry their shapes
by violence and time;
an engine crossing,
re-crossing salt water, hauling
immigrants and the junk
of the poor. These
are the faces I love, the bodies
and scents of bodies
for which I long
in various ways, at various times,
thirteen gathered around the redwood,
happy, talkative, voracious
at day's end,
eager to eat
four kinds of meat
prepared four different ways,
numerous plates and bowls of rice and vegetables,
each made by distinct affections
and brought to table by many hands.

Brothers and sisters by blood and design,
who sit in separate bodies of varied shapes,
we constitute a many-membered
body of love.
In a world of shapes
of my desires, each one here
is a shape of one of my desires, and each
is known to me and dear by virtue
of each one's unique corruption
of those texts, the face, the body:
that jut jaw

to gnash tendon;
that wide nose to meet the blows
a face like that invites;
those long eyes closing on the seen;
those thick lips
to suck the meat of animals
or recite 300 poems of the T'ang;
these teeth to bite my monosyllables;
these cheekbones to make
those syllables sing the soul.
Puffed or sunken
according to the life,
dark or light according
to the birth, straight
or humped, whole, manqué, quasi, each pleases, verging
on utter grotesquery.
All are beautiful by variety.
The soul too
is a debasement
of a text, but, thus, it
acquires salience, although a
human salience, but
inimitable, and, hence, memorable.
God is the text.

The soul is a corruption
and a mnemonic.

A bright moment,
I hold up an old head
from the sea and admire the haughty
down-curved mouth
that seems to disdain
all the eyes are blind to,
including me, the eater.
Whole unto itself, complete
without me, yet its

shape complements the shape of my mind.
I take it as text and evidence
of the world's love for me,
and I feel urged to utterance,
urged to read the body of the world, urged
to say it
in human terms,
my reading a kind of eating, my eating
a kind of reading,
my saying a diminishment, my noise
a love-in-answer.
What is it in me would
devour the world to utter it?
What is it in me will not let
the world be, would eat
not just this fish,
but the one who killed it,
the butcher who cleaned it.
I would eat the way he
squats, the way he
reaches into the plastic tubs
and pulls out a fish, clubs it, takes it
to the sink, guts it, drops it on the weighing pan.

I would eat that thrash
and plunge of the watery body
in the water, that liquid violence
between the man's hands,
I would eat
the gutless twitching on the scales,
three pounds of dumb
nerve and pulse, I would eat it all
to utter it.
The deaths at the sinks, those bodies prepared
for eating, I would eat,
and the standing deaths
at the counters, in the aisles,

the walking deaths in the streets,
the death-far-from-home, the death-
in-a-strange-land, these Chinatown
deaths, these American deaths.
I would devour this race to sing it,
this race that according to Emerson
managed to preserve to a hair
for three or four thousand years
the ugliest features in the world.
I would eat these features, eat
the last three or four thousand years, every hair.
And I would eat Emerson, his transparent soul, his
soporific transcendence.
I would eat this head,
glazed in pepper-speckled sauce,
the cooked eyes opaque in their sockets.
I bring it to my mouth and—
the way I was taught, the way I've watched
others do before me do—
with a stiff tongue lick out
the cheek-meat and the meat
over the armored jaw, my eating,
its sensual, salient nowness,
punctuating the void
from which such hunger springs and to which it proceeds.

And what
is this
I excavate
with my mouth?
What is this
plated, ribbed, hinged
architecture, this *carp head*,
but one more
articulation of a single nothing
severally manifested?
What is my eating,

rapt as it is,
but another
shape of going,
my immaculate expiration?

O, nothing is so
steadfast it won't go
the way the body goes.
The body goes.
The body's grave,
so serious
in its dying,
arduous as martyrs
in that task and as
glorious. It goes
empty always
and announces its going
by spasms and groans, farts and sweats.

What I thought were the arms
aching *cleave*, were the knees trembling *leave*.
What I thought were the muscles
insisting *resist, persist, exist,*
were the pores
hissing *mist* and *waste*.
What I thought was the body humming *reside, reside,*
was the body sighing *revise, revise.*
O, the murderous deletions, the keening
down to nothing, the cleaving.
All of the body's revisions end
in death.
All of the body's revisions end.

Bodies eating bodies, heads eating heads,
we are nothing eating nothing,
and though we feast,
are filled, overfilled,

we go famished.
We gang the doors of death.
That is, our deaths are fed
that we may continue our daily dying,
our bodies going
down, while the plates-soon-empty
are passed around, that true
direction of our true prayers,
while the butcher spells
his message, manifold,
in the mortal air.
He coaxes, cleaves, brings change
before our very eyes, and at every
moment of our being.
As we eat we're eaten.
Else, what is this
violence, this salt, this
passion, this heaven?

I thought the soul an airy thing.
I did not know the soul
is cleaved so that the soul might be restored.
Live wood hewn,
its sap springs from a sticky wound.
No seed, no egg has he
whose business calls for an axe.
In the trade of my soul's shaping,
he traffics in hews and hacks.

No easy thing, violence.
One of its names? Change. Change
resides in the embrace
of the effaced and the effacer,
in the covenant of the opened and the opener;
the axe accomplishes it on the soul's axis.
What then may I do
but cleave to what cleaves me.

I kiss the blade and eat my meat.
I thank the wielder and receive,
while terror spirits
my change, sorrow also.
The terror the butcher
scripts in the unhealed
air, the sorrow of this Shang
dynasty face. African face with slit eyes. He is
my sister, this
beautiful Bedouin, this Shulamite,
keeper of Sabbaths, diviner
of holy texts, this dark
dancer, this Jew, this Asian, this one
with the Cambodian face, Vietnamese face, this Chinese
I daily face,
this immigrant,
this man with my own face.

1990

THE ETERNAL SON

Someone's thinking about his mother tonight.

The wakeful son
of a parent who hardly sleeps,

the sleepless father of his own
restless child, God, is it you?
Is it me? Do you have a mother?

Who mixes flour and sugar
for your birthday cake?

Who stirs slumber and remembrance
in a song for your bedtime?

If you're the cry enjoining dawn,
who birthed you?

If you're the bell tolling night
without circumference, who rocked you?

Someone's separating
the white grains of insomnia
from the black seeds
of his sleep.

If it isn't you, God, it must be me.

My mother's eternal son,
I can't hear the rain without thinking
it's her in the next room
folding our clothes to lay inside a suitcase.

And now she's counting her money
on the bed, the good paper
and the paper from the other country
in separate heaps.

If day comes soon, she could buy our passage.
But if our lot is the rest of the night,
we'll have to trust unseen hands
to hand us toward ever deeper sleep.

Then I'll be the crumb
at the bottom of her pocket,
and she can keep me
or sow me on the water,
as she pleases. Anyway,

she has too much to carry, she who knows
night must tell the rest of every story.

Now she's wondering about the sea.
She can't tell if the white foam laughs
I was born dark! while it spins
opposite the momentum of our dying,

or do the waves journey beyond
the name of every country
and the changing color of her hair.

And if she's weeping,
it's because she's misplaced
both of our childhoods.

And if she's humming, it's because
she's heard the name of life:
A name, but no name, the dove

bereft of memory and finally singing
how the light happened
to one who gave up
ever looking back.

2001

Laura Mullen

Laura Mullen was born in Los Angeles, California, in 1958. She received her MFA degree from the Iowa Writers Workshop and currently teaches at Louisiana State University in Baton Rouge. The author of _The Surface_, _After I Was Dead_, and _Subject_, Mullen's work combines a fierce attraction to experimental poetics with a concrete desire not to slip into pedantic meaninglessness; that is, she wants her poetry to engage the vanguard of contemporary American practice with a wit which undercuts the often overly self-assured posture of such theory. Energetic and original, Mullen has also written two hybrid texts, _The Tales of Horror_ and _Murmur_ —which, like her poetry, similarly grapple with narrative conventions. Her writing has won many awards, including a fellowship from the National Endowment for the Arts.

WHITE PAINTINGS I

My lips are zippered shut.
I need distracting.
I've changed my mind: my face
Is boarded up like a house.
I'm nailed shut, it's got to be
"Like" something. Like life
Is happening and not happening—
Is happening too slowly
And too fast, because you can't
Stop it. You see your hands
Coming off the wheel, trying
To put something in between
Your face and your fate and
You hear yourself screaming.
What was it you heard yourself
Singing? *How did* "I" *get here?*
The force of the impact
Slammed us together. In school
We had a little song, we lined up
Neatly. In the open mouths
Someone dropped a coin.
Some coins. Breaking my fists
On this glass and then asphalt there is no
History, I said, meaning I don't want
To be touched. Now you've closed
The eye-flaps, you must want
Forgiveness. These layers
Are great: this white, off-white
And off-off-white in a dense
Application, but I feel like the latex
Is tearing. I hear the sirens—
Please don't try to move me—
I'm tasting the metal teeth: admitting
Everything's finished between us,
Or nearly, singing it over the rim

Of the lifted glass, mouth full of belated
Apologies; a clear fluid—spilling back out
Through the seams *(Completely,* you said,
Untranslatable)—escaping.

1996

WHITE PAINTINGS II

(in parenthesis)

So what if I scar?
I got my skin to yield up its secrets.
I know how everything is
Inside: suspended, contingent.
I take the knowledgeable risk.
I follow the loop to the final
Destination. I come again
To the part
Where I'm making the first
Cut, where I'm breaking
And entering,
Where I'm walking in
And taking the gloves off.
I watch it like a film.
Quiet in the audience.
I like these marks. Each time
Could be the first, if only
I didn't keep track, if only
There wasn't always more
Resistance in the surface
Where the badly healed
Silence twists in broken
Lines, livid and thick.
It seems that everything
Depends on something else:
It seems that everything
Wants out. It's a system.
So it hurts. I'm not surprised
I try to escape. Room
To move is room
To flee in, or
All movement is flight.
It's a system. It just takes time
To get used to it. I like to watch
The thing in action. Lights.

Camera. That first cut, I love it
When I squirm like that—
I'm all over these sheets—
But I'm disappointed,
Too. What can I say?
I expected more of myself.
All movement is attempted
Flight, and useless.
This is what happens, I say,
Trying to shove it all back
In some kind of order, trying
To remember how everything
Went *before*—positioned
In reference—looking for some
Epiphany to liberate, to take
Away on parole, at least:
This is what happens to you
When you don't cooperate;
This is what happens to you
When you refuse to talk.

1996

WHITE PAINTINGS III

Another funeral.
The glare from the open
Coffin throwing the mourners'
Shadows onto that shifting wall
Of insects so we are
Embroidered on the night.
They seethe, we seethe.
You no longer move at all
Insofar as we understand
Movement. Light
Seeping out like milk: the light
At least, escaping. To begin
With guilt. The faces of the other
Mourners tense—past
And present "relationships,"
Lips moving, voices lost,
Wondering just how long—
Reflecting my own face?
To start over again, sorry.
This summer-weight
Black wool soaked through,
The sour river-scented
Air sluggishly swaying
These broken off
Green threads the sick weeping
Willow's hanging onto
"For dear life?"
It isn't so late as all that,
Though we're, most of us,
By now, more than half
Memory, scrambled and
Unquiet (buzz, buzz)
Trying to weave you—
Stiff and unworkable—

Back in or at least mend
The tear in the fabric.
We know by now there isn't
Going to be enough
Time to finish it.
The wavering drone
Of these voices not
The music you wanted—
That doesn't exist yet.

1996

WHITE PAINTINGS IV

(Independence Day)

1.

Above the banks of fog the muffled thud
Of rockets—I remember—never seen,
But we stood there for awhile, *en famille,* looking up
At nothing. Intermittently brightening
And dimming, blank blanket above an airport
Built to test the instruments and abilities
Of those attempting to take off, or land, in this—
Thick whitish, murky soup, confusion—sightless.
Thud. Thud. Like something dead
Still being kicked. I don't need to add
What I add: *hollow, meaningless.* We piled
Back into the car and probably
Our father drove us home again,
If he wasn't already blind drunk.

2.

The unbroken wall of your silence, behind which: ghosts
And shadows, thin shapes in constant, shifiting, flight.
The most intense of intimacies and then complete
Absence….Unable to tell you even the first thing about it:
How I was out in the garden of ashes, the garden I painted
Completely white in the middle of summer, the garden of doors
Going nowhere, brought out of doors to be painted
And taken back into the house untouched because I never
Got around to it, not in time for the celebration; how I found myself
Out of doors in the sticky heat, one of the "grown ups,"
In the green depths of a garden I'd only imagined
Painting white, I'd named "of ashes," drinking *blanc de blancs*
Until there were two of each guest I tried to make
Merge when they were speaking, carefully shutting one painted
Eyelid…: how the voices seemed to come from far away
And stay there…—I have no memory of what we talked about.

1996

WHITE PAINTINGS V

I put my hands through your head.
But you never offered me
Any resistance. I put my arms
Through your body. I end up
Holding myself. I say *Somebody*
Please get me through this
Part—as though it were only a part. You
Disperse. You always disperse.
I walk through *You* like a doorway
In a structure made entirely of fog,
Set out on the edge of a cliff. "Falling
In love again…"? I walk in and out
Of us both. The letters I start
Break off, start over (*Somebody,*
Please…), accumulate, becoming a body
Of work, aborted: fetus and corpse.
I try to read everything I possibly can
Into the silences: to see—
For "next time"–how it's my fault.
Where was the railing? The warning
Sign? The flimsy excuse? This stuff
Can't be grasped. I'm trying to tell you
Exactly what it's like to be this
Lonely and frightened. I put my face
Through your face. On this side
It seems our eyes are wet—
But that doesn't change anything.
Our "grief"? Even that will get
Taken apart. The walls of the building
Are covered with advertisements
For everything I ever thought
I wanted: in the shredded white
Skin sloughing off I still make out
The stuttered remains of wild
Suggestions and pleas, desperate

Ideas about happiness. I try
To re-imagine myself, free at last
Of your interpretations. I put
My hand out into the empty
Space it seems your hand could be,
If only I were somebody else: it fits
'Like a glove,' like it was made for me.
I put my fist through the glass.

1996

Lucia Perillo

Lucia Perillo was born in 1958 in New York City. In 1986, she received an MA in creative writing from Syracuse University. A 2000 recipient of a prestigious MacArthur Fellowship, Perillo is the author of four books of poetry, *Dangerous Life*, *The Body Mutinies*, *The Oldest Map with the Name America*, and, most recently, *Luck is Luck*. Her poetry frequently uses a long line in order to capaciously accommodate a variety of materials: rumination, narrative threads, contemporary and classical culture, all mixed dashingly in poems driven by a sassy yet speculative and sensitive voice. She has taught at Southern Illinois University, Saint Martin's University, and Warren Wilson College. She now lives in Washington State where, before becoming a professor, she worked as a ranger at Mount Rainier National Park.

The Destruction of the Mir

Every night space junk falls from the sky—
usually a titanium fuel tank. Usually falling
into the ocean, or into nowhere in particular
because we are a planet of great vacancies,
never mind how much fog would be required
in downtown Tokyo. In the Skylab days
you'd see people on the streets wearing iron
helmets, like centurions. But nowadays
we go bare-headed, as if to say to the heavens:
Wake me when I am someone else.
Like the man whose car made fast acquaintance
with what Yeats would have called the bole of a tree.
And who now believes he has written
many of the latest hits, which he will sing
for you while he splits a cord of wood:
like a virgin—whap!—like a virgin—whap!—
until he's got enough fuel for the winter
and a million dollars stashed in an offshore bank.
You may think it's tragic, like my Buddhist friend
who claims that any existence means suffering,
though my gay friend says: phooey, what about
Oscar night, what about making popcorn
and wrapping up with your sweetie
in that afghan your great-aunt made long ago?
You don't have to dwell on the fact that she's dead
or bring up her last unkempt year in the home
when she'd ask anyone who walked in the door
to give her a good clunk on the head. Instead
what about her crocheting these squares
in preposterous colors, orange and green,
though why must their clashing be brought to the fore
if the yarn was enough to keep her happy?
In fact don't the clashes light the sparks

in this otherwise corny thing? Which is safer
to make than a hole in the skull to let out
the off-gassing of one's bad spirits.
As in trephination performed by the Incas
who traded their melancholy for a helmet
made from a turtle shell. You never know
when your brain will require such armor—
could happen sometime when you least expect.
Could even happen when you are parked
behind your desk, where a very loud thump
makes you look up to discover a robin
diving into the window again and again.
It is spring after all, and in its reflection
the bird may have found the perfect mate:
thus doth desire propel us headlong
toward the smash. Don't even try
translating glass into bird-speak—it only knows
it wants the one who dropped from sight.
Same one who beaned it, same one who's perched,
glaring back from a bough of the Japanese maple
with its breast fit to burst. And behind the lace
of new leaves, there's a wallpaper of clouds
weighing hundreds of tons
but which float nonetheless—
in the blue sky that seemed to fit so well
when we first strapped it on our heads.

2002

La Deuxieme Sexe

The famous Polish poet calls Simone de Beauvoir a Nazi hag
but to me she will always be her famous book,
the one with the Matisse paper cut on the cover,
a sad blue nude I took into the woods.
Where we college girls went to coax the big picture
from her, as if she could tell us how to use
all the strange blades on our Swiss army knives—
the firewood we arranged in either log cabin or tipi,
a little house built to be burned down.
Which could be a metaphor:
Simone as the wind puffing the damp flames,
a cloud with a mouth that became obsolete
once we started using gasoline. Still,
she gave me one lesson that sticks, which is:
do not take a paperback camping in the rain
or it may swell to many times its original size,
and if you start with a big book you'll end up
with a cinderblock. In that vein I pictured Simone as huge
until (much later) I read that her size was near-midget—
imagine, if we took Gertrude Stein, we'd be there still,
trying to build some kind of travois to drag her body out.
The other thing I remember: a word, *immanence*—
meaning, you get stuck with the cooking and laundry
while the man gets to hit on all your friends in Paris.
Sure you can put the wet book in the oven
and try baking it like a cake. But the seam will stay soggy
even when the pages rise, ruffled like French pastry.
As far as laundry goes, it's best I steer clear,
what with my tendency to forget the tissues
wadded in my sleeves. What happens is
I think I'm being so careful, and everything
still comes out like the clearing where we woke.

Covered in white flakes that were then the real thing:
snow. Which sounds more la-di-da in French.
But then the sun came up and all *la neige* vanished
like those chapters we grew bored with and had skipped.

2002

Urban Legend

Like many stories, this one begins with Jesus—
well he sure looks like Jesus, this guy pulled over by the ditch.
Let's say the tarp has blown off the back of his Isuzu pickup.
Let's say that the apostles are slowly rising heavenward.

See them twisting in the thermals, in this sky that's not a joke
even if these fugitives could figure in a gag's protracted set-up.
Calling for the hauling of twelve helium-filled desire dolls—
to a toga party. See how the apostles all have boners underneath
          their robes.

And isn't that like me, to put the *boners* into play,
however inappropriate, when this is not a joke.
This is not a joke because the story wants to go into the record.
Yes it does want. The story has a little mind that thinks.

And the mind sends its ambassadors: these poodles nuked in
          microwaves,
bonsai kittens, sewer crocodiles, rats suckled in maternity wards.
I believe in the fatal hairdo just for the love of saying *fatal hairdo*.
And I believe in the stolen kidney because I too have woken up with
     something missing.

But I haven't spoken yet of the rapture, another word whose saying
is like dancing at a toga party after downing many shots.
Who hasn't tried to pull their arms from the sleeves of gravity's lead coat?
Who doesn't have at least one pair of wax wings out in the garage?

So back to Jesus, back to daylight, and you can make the dimwit me
who launches herself into the updraft of the rapture
and goes sailing straight through the story's sunroof. Above, the bonsai
     kittens
pad the sky as cherubim. Below me, hairdos right and left are going up in
     smoke.

Now the apostles are storming heaven, the Isuzu's motor's ticking
while the left hand of Jesus forms a ledge above his brow.
And you, earth angel, fear not my crash landing in the diamond lane—
the vinyl men are full of noble gas, and I'm rising on my balsa wings.

2002

FOR THE PILEATED WOODPECKER AND ITS COUSIN, THE IVORY-BILLED, WHO MAY OR MAY NOT BE EXTINCT

So ta-*dah*: here's the moment to which we've been brung —
but right off the bat, don't things get snarled.
"The moment" feels right, but I'm not sure about *brung*,
a folksy idiom to brush against the modern, which is our way,
the modern way, you know:
the old barn parked beside the SUV.
Or the pitchfork the parent stabs through the game boy.
The salt pork completely savaged by the microwave.
That's what's wrong with the moment, it is always so shiny
when it pulls up like a white limo at the curb.
Or to use a supporting argument
from inside the Toyota by the Skokomish River
where Jim says: "What would you call that giant woodpecker?"
and I say: "What giant woodpecker?" but poof:
the bird has flown before I can fix it
(the vision of it, the real of it) with any sort of toxic nimbus
from the aerosol can with the ball inside it, ticking.
Other times I've heard its knocking,
the loud hard gavel of *momentmomentmoment*
but in the woods I tracked down just a feathery blur, a black wig flying.
And was it only a moment ago I was dressed so chic
and now I'm taking those same clothes to the thrift store
in plastic bags, like a body being dumped?
One night I even performed the experiment
of looking into the mirror and saying the word *now*,
only the now that was said was the now that was gone
and did I feel it? could I feel it?
Here's what happens: the tongue knocks on the palate
before lying down in the jaw's own swamp,
then the *ow*-sound flies from the nest of the throat
and the self ends up a doofus, standing there
breathing with an open mouth.

2002

SHRIKE TREE

Most days back then I would walk by the shrike tree,
a dead hawthorn at the base of a hill.
The shrike had pinned smaller birds on the tree's black thorns
and the sun had stripped them of their feathers.

Some of the dead ones hung at eye level
while some burned holes in the sky overhead.
At least it is honest,
the body apparent
and not rotting in the dirt.

And I, having never seen the shrike at work,
can only imagine how the breasts were driven into the branches.
When I saw him he'd be watching from a different tree
with his mask like Zorro
and the gray cape of his wings.

At first glance he could have been a mockingbird or a jay
if you didn't take note of how his beak was hooked.
If you didn't know the ruthlessness of what he did—
ah, but that is a human judgment.

They are mute, of course, a silence at the center of a bigger silence,
these rawhide ornaments, their bald skulls showing.
And notice how I've slipped into the present tense
as if they were still with me.

Of course they are still with me.

They hang there, desiccating
by the trail where I walked back when I could walk,
before life pinned me on its thorn.
It is ferocious, life, but it must eat
then leaves us with the artifact.

Which is: these black silhouettes in the midday sun
strict and jagged, like an Asian script.
A tragedy that is not without its glamour.
Not without the runes of the wizened meat.

Because imagine the luck!—: to be plucked from the air,
to be drenched and dried in the sun's bright voltage—
well, hard luck is luck, nonetheless.
With a chunk of sky in each eye socket.
And the pierced heart strung up like a pearl.

2002

Bin Ramke

Bin Ramke was born in Port Neches, Texas, in 1947. A prolific poet, Bin Ramke's most recent book is *Airs, Waters, Places*. Other recent titles include *Wake* and *Massacre of the Innocents*. Recipient of the Yale Younger Poet's Award for his first book of poetry, Ramke has served as editor for *The Denver Quarterly* and the University of Georgia Press. Author of a dark and invigorating poetry that explores the boundaries of formal conventions of line, syntax, and speaker, Ramke's obsessive confrontation of epistemological and ethical questions has shaped especially vivid work in the last three books. He is a professor of English at the University of Denver.

LIKE ULYSSES

I read by the afternoon light then hope
to sleep through the end of the century.
Constantly embarrassed by sneezes I was
allergic to everything. The lines
of sunlight through the dust of local
demolition drove me inward, a leopard
looking for some lamb to lie down with.
"Oh modern modes of loneliness" I would groan.
"Oh searing attitudes of largesse, Oh
fulsome days of good country air." Meanwhile
there is a continent whose men disembowel
themselves and any handy captive monkey
just for sport. Somewhere children
choke on bits of cheese and candy
simply for the pattern they see sprawling
at sunset. And somewhere the various
rounds of randomness live like choirs
of angels. You know what it is to have friends
and to be unhappy in the style of the period
(Louis Ferdinand-Céline), to collapse into
an ecstasy of defilement, when you have the cash,
or to recall that little coin of bread
the priest would place with his own clean
hand on the pillow of your little tongue,
all clean from brushing that morning
and rinsing without taste, without a swallow.
Homemade sacraments are best,
how the balls on the pool table for years
made their complicated little rounds,
into the nine little holes then back
to the green fabulous felt oh miles of travel
circumscribed, domestic and dangerous.

1995

ART, LOVE, GEOLOGY

Ist es schon, in der sonne zu gehn.
—*Trakl*

Here is a little book of instructions. It says care
must be taken. For instance, a form of health as a
version of vanity (as when a poor stonecutter set up
shop to live off the vanity of travelers, pioneers
who stopped to scratch names and dates in inviting surfaces
but granite is hard on the amateur so a graffitist,

                 *

an American artist, against the rapacious
rock body of the earth did cover the good body with
American names, this national poetry which must be
written carelessly before the one war, after the other.
The view was magnificent, and the air smelled of the future)
Vanity in this world, my Dear, your hair the color,
this kind of poetry, this world tells itself stories,
O famous your green shoes your fabulous wishes your
hair the color of tea and your green shoes aren't you something.
It says here you must listen to your own history, it says
you must take care, and it says here you must pronounce
your name, your own name here _____

                 *

This man did believe in the monochrome
possibilities, the way the camera once would focus
such a narrow range of color thus the *sharpness*
of the old photographs, the clarity of vision
of the American West before the development
of panchromatic films. And the movies, the cow-
boys and Indians blazing black and white.

                 *

"At the edge of the forest/Stillness encounters
a dark deer"—the way she said it, my friend
said it of Trakl, his poem. *Geistliche Dammerung*
and it is snowing now and cold. When I knew her
we were young and the age of the earth indeterminate.
Forests had edges. Deer were a species of Indian.

*

Here is the world come to comfort me. Here
is a child come to follow me home.

*

The traveling salesman said to the farmer's daughter:
we are in this world together and there is no place
to sleep, so let's join hands and sing of the glory
and honor of the forest and its deer which watch us;
see their eyes reflect the light, see them wait for us.

*

Und rings erglanzten Hugel and Wald.

*

And surrounding us, you and I, love,
something like the night—at least it is dark,
at least it is silent. It seems to move
only when we do not look at it. It seems
to be the world, but who knows, and we,
do we really care more for each other
than for the world, can the songs be right?

*

Surrounding shimmering in ultraviolet
the darkness to eyes not our own, but we
have gauges to measure this shimmer.
The insects see in light not ours
the insects see flowers in violet so deep
its darkness shimmers in the corner of
my eye as if I made it up.

*

If hills emerge too slowly to see, still, evidence
remains—it's what geology says, that this earth
moves beneath each lover, slow and impossible
but there you have it, the hills rise around us
when we are not looking and one day an alp
taps you on the shoulder as you kiss
and your mind wasn't on time; it is late.

*

This is the forest, here, we live here. Arboreal
safety. Who cares for evolution. Here, let me
love you and then we'll fall from the trees like
fruit, the sound it makes, the forest surrounds
our racial despair. Oh how we hate to be human.

1995

ENTER CELIA, WITH A WRITING

You have said; but whether wisely or no, let the forest judge
We continue to attend to truth as we see it.
We are a small group of humans, full of good
intentions. We are full of despair.
We continue to read ourselves to sleep at night.
We live through the nights full of desolate desire.
We have kitchens and small animals for company.
We are as good as any, better than some.
We have thought about our lives, and now it is dawn.

                    *

dans mon pays, on ne questionne pas un homme emu
(In my country, we are discreet around men in tears;
in my homeland, we observe the decorum of private grief;
back where I was born, men did not show their feelings;
surely you will not disturb me in my hour of anguish.)

The French, or such Frenchman as that, fill their dawns
with angry art and intricate analysis. It is a way to be,
and certainly you yourself could learn something:
for instance, what of the dead Father you never buried,
and the Mother you will not allow to die? Won't
you accept his good advice, his friendship?

And what do you know about Mr. Char
and his little poems whose delicate directions
might also say with him *Les branches sont libres*
de n'avoir pas de fruits (and if the branches of my trees
are thusly liberated, why not call it triumph, why
not eat? No nation is more hungry than the French.)

                    *

Is it not my fault. Blame yourself, this art
is not what it used to be. We grow old in debt
and no child smiles when we fall apart

no child ever sees it happen. They dangle
their charms in front of each other, they burn
with a hard, gemlike flame. The acute angle
of their anger dissipates the affection of poor
parents—they never say thank you—and the parks
are full of their demons arranger flowers fewer

care about each year. When was a rose
last named for a poet? Who cares for art
unless on stage, whose child knows

how to do anything small and discreet?
Not that it matters: all small wars wither
into family, and the State weeps in the streets.

1999

Famous Poems of the Past Explained

Imagine how much I hope, imagine
what a fan I am, how I want to read
wisdom, yes, and applaud such confidence.
I was about to step when I noticed
there was no world there, so I turned
quickly searching for foot-sized solidarity
to enhance my belief in the future.
Then I noticed the little yellow flowers
that sprang timely in my footprints

impressions graceful and slender as a past.
Another time you were with me and we
were young it had to do with sex
we breathed heavily the hard air
and saw our own internal shapes turn white
in front of us then fade into the borrowed
dusk of the room. It was perhaps
our first time, and I was in love
with your bravery, how you fearlessly

gave yourself into yourself, so I gathered
a small nosegay of yellow violets
that were the color of the bed
and of the dust floating languorous.
And then the barest small foot of you
kept creeping into my memory, as if
I had seen you naked and unafraid, as
each tiny foot of yours impressed itself
in the snow and the white nativity

of the season turned itself sorrowful
but so attractively. No one knew better
than you the look of the afternoon,
and how the foot is slim and of a shape
to win a woman's greatest ease and note that

the memory fades, and I pay my bill
and walk home past the flower shops.
Orpheus tracing his steps back to the surface
to make music again; how the instrument

is a body of wood breathing, a wisdom of
will and carpentry given voice; how he knew
tunes to turn trees into audience. Anyway,
the little family in the church held their dirty hymnals
and sang the old songs to the wheezing
box behind them. Nobody thought about anything
much: hunger, horror, the grand harmonies
of the light, the night where nothing
but blossoms of stars would crowd

and tumultuous clouds came pouring
over the rim from Canada
tendering the shiny coin of rain upon the plain:
Let not the darke thee cumber;
What thought the Moon do's slumber?
            the starres of the night
         will lend thee their light,
like Tapers cleare without number.

1999

Thou Hast Blessed the Work of His Hands

He was the one who would not use his face—
would keep it in reserve, would use his hands,
one at a time, alternately. Would use feet.

Would be happy when it suited, would
mourn when required. Such a poem as was
needed, he would make. Would want,

when those he loves are in pain,
to be. There. To bleed for all equally.
And here was a thing to believe: "to live whole

lives with littleness, how tired it makes us,
a sharp fear, this point to which the eye was
drawn—defames then defeats the hand—an agony

it is to follow self into its shameful needs" and
so forth. "Wherever you can: count" said
Francis Galton. We do not know most things.

I might know a few things. I can
rarely tell the difference. Where there are flocks
of Monk Parakeets, Green Neighbors, they rouse

us to collect feathers under streetlights
on nightly walks where are builded unsightly nests.
A dozen wild parakeets in furious formation fly

across the park swerve to streak past, accidental, me.
Pyromancy, a method of augury by reading
weblike patterns which appear on bone surface

following the application of heat, especially
favored in China—but what did it sound like
when the bone cracked, its surface crazed?

The sound of the word "sound," as in "the sound
of young girls." Or "the voices in my head."
Complex looking, calligraphically.

Among things to love in this world are eyelet fabrics,
suggestive nests of absence promising
a glimpse of flesh and remembrance of touch,

of the feel of the young world.
The skin beneath the fabric shines—
Wann was a word for it, for gloss or sheen; *Fealo*

meant glint, the sparkle of sun, say, on waves;
while *lux* meant the source of light, *color*
the effect of that light on a surface, as of

the moistening skin beneath the eyelets.
Lumen, the ray of light traveling between
the surface and the eye, the source and

the surface; *splendor* was the word for
that final reflected, lustrous quality,
that which draws the hand inexorable.

"The winds sweeping the surface
of the waters diminish them, as does
the ethereal sun unraveling them

by his rays." *De Rerum Natura* 5, 390.
When an electron "moves" to a higher orbit
it does not move but merely is now elsewhere—

once it was here, now it is there. This is not
possible in the old world where I used to live
by manufacture. The new world is one of

probabilities, where numbers add up
and the glint of sun on flesh is ephemeral.
All is diminished in his world, yet all the more

unaccountably glorious. We love it all,
and each the other, or so it seems. His hands
cracked a sound a second face fallen.

2003

Donald Revell

Donald Revell was born in 1954 in the Bronx, New York. He received his PhD from SUNY Buffalo in 1980. Drawing from diverse sources, including French surrealism, American mystical and antinomian thought, poststructuralist theory, and various musical forms, Revell's poetry exhibits both radical experimentation and a deep connection to American traditions. From Anne Hutchinson to Thoreau to Charles Ives, exploration of the unsayable and the erased have engaged Revell's thought and found expression in his work. Revell's first book, *From the Abandoned Cities*, was selected for publication in the 1982 National Poetry Series. Since then, he has published seven additional books of poetry, including *New Dark Ages*, *Erasures*, and *My Mojave*. He has also published a translation of the French poet Guillame Apollinaire's *Alcools*. Revell presently teaches at the University of Utah.

How Passion Comes to Matter

When I was a boy, my father drove us once
very fast along a road deep in a woodland.
The leaves on the trees turned into mirrors
signaling with bright lights frantically.
They said it was the end of the world and to go faster.

I am beginning to know in whose name
the uprisings, the sudden appearances
of facades like damp cloths, somehow happen.
Think, for me, of a woman thrown
in front of a train. You can see her

falling in the staccato of her last gesture,
that little wave, and she will never stop
leaving you, just as you will never find
a kiss that can move faster than a train.
Or think, rather, of a boy

who felt the death inside his first lover
and went home and died of gunshot in his sleep.
I know there is a cult of such things—the young dead.
I understand the excess they cause.
But as passion is their signature, admit

we are grief-sodden and thus romantic.
We raise no columns in the great style but only
the anxious facades of left-wing cities
never to be completed. She brings
a damaged son and an open mouthful of milk

to one who is always leaving her and she
reappears suddenly under the low and inwrought
housefronts of April, that month teeming
with slaughter. It is the pause of the world.
Time triumphs in an incompleteness we can feel

on each other's bedding. In the unstill noise
of couples, high, shameless operas prove
the truth of uprisings, guiltless trains, gunshots
in a boy's sleep. Father drove us very fast.
In left-wing cities, we can drive no faster.

1990

LAST

The unsigned architecture of loneliness
is becoming taller, finding a way farther
above the horizontal flowering
of the Cold War, the peonies
and star asters of wild partisanship.
I have a shambling gait and lonely
hysteria, but no Terror. I am free
to shamble past the vacant lot of my son's
conception, to shamble past the bar where I
conceived adultery as a Terror
that would be endless, flowering
in great waves through air striated like chenille.
I walk for a long time and try to conjure
elsewhere in its early isolation.
I cannot. It is all redestinated
by the future like the loose balloons
a janitor recovers at 6 AM
from cold light fixtures. The Cold War is ending.
Buildings are taller and have no names.

I.

The romance of every ideology
torments the romance of another. How
beautifully, in the beginning, in
the gale and embrace of isolation, boys
capered over a shambles and swore oaths.
The scent of urine in the hall at home
was righteousness. The beautiful nude
obscured by dust in a paperweight
was righteousness. Neglectful townships coming
into steep flower just as boys were flowering
needed the correction of righteousness,
the horizontal slag of government
by children. Only the insane allegiances
endure. The mad counterparts are lovers

passion cannot explain nor circumstance
restrict to the dead zones of irony.
A counterpart of the end of the Cold War
is adultery. A counterpart
of loving a divided Berlin
unto death is fatherhood, the doting
maintenance of sons in vacant lots
continuing the wars of rubble
for righteousness' sake and for the sake
of nudes obscured by dust and vulgarity.

Romance torments romance. The most beautiful
moment of the twentieth century
galed and embraced the acrid smoky air
as the Red Army entered Berlin
as Hitler shriveled in the gasoline fire
as Red Army flags opened above Berlin
safeguarding the ruins of a changeless future.
Townships blackened even as they flowered.
Loose balloons cluttered the low sky and sun.
I walked for a long time and tried to conjure
the form of kindness. It was a domestic
animal confused in the tall grass.
Boys set fire to the grass. History
that opens flags opened the fire,
and Berlin, divided from Berlin,
began to love its children past all reason.

2.

My son reads sermons of pain and writes on walls.
He starves the ground
he walks on, preparing a dead city
to be worthy of its new flags, to shine
as exploded windows shine, raining down
for hours after the wrecking crews have gone.
I have a lover now who hates children.

The hatred floats inside of her, a weightless
sexual pavilion of perfect form
and perfect emptiness. I thought
by making love to her I would conceive
nothing but Terror, outrage upon outrage,
a violence that would last my whole life
and free my son. I was ignorant as a balloon.
Across the luminous expressway, I see
the shapes of charred tenements castellated,
fading into the more tender shapes of night.
It may be the last night in history. Tomorrow
pulls down the Berlin wall, pulls down my honor,
and I return to my lover's bed to float
in a white condom, no longer my son's father.
Tomorrow describes everything in detail.
It explains nothing. It does not teach my boy
that tenements are better than the future,
better than peace, more likely to produce
brothers than are the glassy hands of mornings
without end or walls denuded of their wire.
In the dead zone of irony before dawn,
only the cats cry, like martyrs in the flame.

   3.

Gates everywhere. The Brandenburg. The Great
Gate of Kiev beneath which children stride
onto an invisible crescendo
disappearing into gasoline fires,
emerging as the new shapes of righteousness
in slow vans through the Brandenburg Gate.
Oaths are secret because none suspects
that they are kept. They thrust themselves towards us
unashamedly, like the insane homeless,
and we do not see them. In our loneliness,
we see a chance for love in betrayal,
not death. In our loneliness, we see the happy

triumph of glassy hands in free elections,
not the denuding of Berlin or wanderings
of children in vans reduced by fire
to black transparencies in the morning shade.
When Joan of Arc surrendered to the flames
she cried out "Jesus, Jesus." Some years later,
a failed magician who loved her cried out
"Joan, Joan" as the flames mocked him with a sortilege
too easy to be unreal or profitable.

I walk for a long time and try to conjure
the form of loneliness without Cold War.
It is ash upon ash, a chiaroscuro
aloft and on the ground, completely still.
Oaths are secret because none suspects
the desperation of every object, the child
in every atom of the misused world
thrust towards us, crying out whatever
sacred name it witnessed put to death
on the ascending music of a wall.
Our buildings are tall and have no names.
The parks grow glassy hands instead of flowers.

4.

Afterwards, the calm is piteous
but insubstantial as a smell of burn
that does not rise in smoke or die with the fire.
Imagine walking out of a house at sunrise
and having to invent air, invent light
from nothing but untriggered memory.
All things beloved are recalled to pain.
Air recollected from the wrists of girls
braceleted for Confirmation, crossed.
Light recollected from between the cars
of night trains in a deep river valley
where islands in the river glowed like swans.
Air recollected from the sex of flowers

in bare rooms, the grainy light of blondes.
Air recollected from religion.
Light recollected from the incensed clutch
of bodies before sunrise in the oaths
of a great and ignorant lost cause.

Imagine walking out of a house at sunrise
having spent the night in bed with a stranger.
Aloft and on the ground the calm
unfurls like flags without device or slogan.
The inconsequence of the day ahead
stirs airless atmospheres in darkness
visible as daylight but without shade.
Without Cold War, without the arbitrary
demarcation of cause from cause, of light
and air from the unsexed improvisations
of memory, I cannot see to walk
or breathe to breathe. Sex becomes applause.
Sex becomes television, and the bastard
avant-garde of lonely architecture
breaks ground at the unwired heart of a city
that marks the capital of nothing now.

5.

A scratchy, recorded call to prayer crosses
the alley from one new building into mine.
The consolations of history are furtive,
then fugitive, then forgotten like a bar
of music that might have been obscene or sacred
once, in another city, in the days
before today. My son is well. He works
the public ground and needs no Antigone.
My lover sits beside him at dinner,
sharing a joke, unmapping the tall future
and its unbiased children, reinventing
the sexual pavilion to accommodate
plague wards. Romance forgives romance.

The early isolation of this gorgeous
century disappears into good works.
The future is best. To put a final stop
to the grotesque unmercy of martyrdom
and to the ruinous armies of mad boys
whose government is rape, whose justice
is a wall, revoke all partisanship,
adjourn the Terror. The future is best.
It unobscures the dusty nudes. It protects
the river islands and their glowing swans.
But when I need to die, who will light the fire?
What names shall I cry out and what music
burn to a black transparency in my heart?
The unborn have been revoked. They will not be kind.

1992

LYRE

Before anything could happen,
flecks of real gold
on her mouth, her eyes more
convex than any others,
the ground spoke, the barrier
of lilacs spoke. What sang
in the black tree was entirely gold.
Her chair was empty.

New absence is a great fugue
dark as the underskin of fruit.
At the center of the earth
it surrounds and amplifies the dead
whose music never slows down.

She came by car. I came by train.
We embraced. It was
at the foot of a hill steeply
crowned with apples
and a ruined fortress.
Imagination did not make the world.

Sweetness is the entire portion.
Before anything could happen,
happiness, the necessary
precondition of the world,
spoke and flowered over the hill.

When I was in Hell
on the ruined palisade,
either mystery or loneliness
kissed my open eyes.

It felt hugely convex, seeing
and immediately forgetting.

By contrast, what I imagined
later was nothing.

1994

FEWER THAN MUSIC

Beloved has found
unseen illustrations
of other situations.
The need to change
rivals the sun.
At least as far
as the nearest mountain
Beloved has found
a fineness still unseen.
Today is fine.
Tomorrow is fine.
With peril through a mountain
Beloved has found
in variation
a last religion.
Stupefied with agreement
it rivals the sun.

1998

Tooms 4

It is a great half world
We were
Not put here
To disturb a spider

We are puppets in the best sense
Panda
Calls from a telephone booth on a desert
Indian reservation to the casino to recover
Her silken jacket forgotten there

Puppets in the best sense
On television
The panda is restored to the wild and dies
On television
The murderer is restored to freedom and kills again

Truth and lies
Enjoy equal eternities

Panda proves it
I sleep on the couch of her approval

It is a great half world
I mourn
Puppeteer Shari Lewis
1933-98 old enough
(Just) to have been my mother
Dying the same day my real mother
Receives the same disease

Panda

40 years ago Shari Lewis made an ageless lamb
Today in lovemaking

I smell sweet of my real mother's
Yellow roses cupped and drooping dead
Mother is on the airplane back to New York City
From Las Vegas where I live

Mourning and disturbance
Make lambs out of human hands alone
No strings

2002

David St. John

David St. John was born in Fresno, California, in 1949. A 1974 graduate of the University of Iowa Writers Workshop, St. John is the author of several books of poetry, including *Hush, No Heaven, Study for the World's Body: New and Selected Poems, The Red Leaves of Night* and, most recently, *The Face: A Novella in Verse.* The lyrical possibilities of the self's encounter with the fallen world have been at the center of David St. John's poetry since his earliest collections. Meticulous attention to sound qualities coupled with a keen sense of tone and dramatic impact—the emotional weight under which his speakers sometimes sing is palpable—are hallmarks of St. John's poetry. His awards include the Rome Fellowship in Literature and a Guggenheim Award; he currently teaches in the English Department at the University of Southern California, Los Angeles.

AFTER ESENIN

Goodbye, old friend, goodbye, goodbye…
The only evidence is my heart.
I lived, they say, & then I died; so what?
In between, just a breath of scarlet smoke.

So goodbye, I know we'll meet again in bed,
But perhaps one much colder & more deep…
When it's said that I grew tired of the world, say, instead
It was the world that first grew tired of me.

1998

ELEGY

It's true such reckless grace should never die,
Just as it's true that death itself is meaningless
To the silver gulls riding the summer sky.

Out of the dust of ancient motorcycle lies,
Beyond the sinless vaudeville one should not confess,
It's true, such a reckless grace should never die

Into some hope that's lifted like an angel's sigh—
Like that black ace hidden in the parrot's vest
As it flies beside the riders of the sky.

So let me wear my anger for a while, my
Last good suit, though I'd feel much better dressed
It's true, wearing your old reckless grace. "Never die,"

You once said to me, "Or else try to surprise
The gods when they're busy fucking; that's more or less
My idea: to go off low-riding a bloody summer sky."

Un coup de des...Les jeux sont faits. I still despise
The empty shadow this last, single die has cast
Along those silver wings lighting the summer sky.
My friend, such reckless grace should never die.

1998

THE OPAL TREES

When I awaken into the dream

Of your body upon my body
I am breathing the fragrant air of
The opal trees where shivering rags
Of light pearlesque the limbs of
Your body upon my body
As I awaken to the moonscape

Of this solitary bed
Still feeling the soft satin of stone
& the blossoms of the opal trees
Littering the sheets of earth beneath me
As their shattered rinds
Swirl through the branches of the dream

Of your body upon my body

2002

SAFFRON

Even the thin tube of Spanish saffron
Sitting on the spice rack above the butcher block
Cooking table seems to glow with the worth
Of at least its weight in gold & today
At the beach a dozen Buddhist monks in golden
Robes stepped out of three limousines
To walk their Holy One out along the dunes

To the water's flayed edge where the sand burned
With a light one could only call in its reddish
Mustard radiance the essence of saffron
& what I remember most of the scent scene as
The Holy One knelt down to touch those waves
Was his sudden laughter & his joy & that
Billowing burnt lemon light opening across the sky

2002

ZUNI RING

Bought a dozen years ago
Hammered silver & set with the stone that baffles
All admirers—sugalite—as dusty as a dark plum
Hung too long on the branch above
The wind-whipped fields a purple just
This side of a bruise its minute rectangular pieces
Inlaid as precisely as a Ravenna mosaic
This devotional band of silver monochrome
I've worn since we walked the yellow lanes of
The pueblo looking for some fetishes of silence
Some relics of adornment we might
Weld to us in the hope that whatever we carried away
Would echo through our bodies like this lightning
Stitching the gathering night.

2002

Dave Smith

Dave Smith was born in Portsmouth, Virginia, in 1942. He is a prolific writer whose poetry, fiction, and criticism form a substantial body of unique work. His books of poetry include *Drunks; Goshawk, Antelope; In the House of the Judge; Cuba Night; Fate's Kite; Tremble*; and *The Wick of Memory: New and Selected Poems 1970-2000*. A forthcoming book, *Little Boats, Unsalvaged*, will be published in 2005. By continually exploring how to conflate the immediacy of the lyric with the meaning found within "a tale," Smith has shaped a lasting body of writing. Winner of a variety of awards—from an NEA grant to a Guggenheim—Smith's impact on contemporary American literature, as an important poet and critic (his collection of criticism, *Local Assays*, is an insightful exploration of the art) is substantial.

THE DREAM OF THE JACKLIGHTER

Because there are no children in his house, there is nothing
to wake to, crying out.
Because he looks like any father and is not. Imagine him,
long snout of the rifle, a shadow, hunting
at night the image of beauty.
His hand on the cold truck-wheel shakes.
His hands in little convulsions
back-lit by gauges and numbers
that stare at him like love's
unremembering eyes.
Because for a man like him there is nothing else but the night
that is beyond the last day.
Because the world arranges such meetings: the deer have come,
they stand as if summoned, in grace.
The cobbled road downspools
under his boots, refusing
to sound like a window opening for the burglar. Light
unalterably leaps from his hand and under it
nothing could change this moment
or blot out the sun-god
laying breath on their breath. Because they wait, cornered
in the walls of his will, believers
mostly in darkness, mostly
not choosers or chosen,
accompanying one appointed, for whom grass at hooves slightly stirs.
Her blue eyes cannot bear him, the shot
rocks her
to buckle under his muzzle.
The fawn would nurse his light except for the throat he slits.
Because he must make his dream real in order to remember some things
cry out in absence and some tearlessly wait.
Because he must violate the world to know
he is in the world.
We are in the world's bed, not sleeping, his name on our lips
drawn from the steadily poured haze of the television.

This is how he enters each house
like a pantomime beside us, trying to show what has passed
beautifully through his hands.
He would like to lie down between us.
Because someone here is the carrier of truth he cannot bear, chosen
for pain he cannot describe but must try to know.
This is a definition of joy and beauty.
Not what you think.
He is not what you think.
He is only something in a dream we are the meaning of, something
we must touch like a deep of water, a scoop snow
in our fists to know how cold we can get.
And beyond everything else this is why
the father will walk into a child's room
at the eve of birth
to sit naked on an icy floor
and think of something
in the world
except light rising from grass—
the stunning light
he must labor for
from that first red pulse ticking like a clock over the fields....

1979

BATS

Still in sleeping bags, the promised delivery
only words as usual, our lives upside down,
we are transients lost in thirteen rooms
built by a judge who died. The landlord says
they mean no harm, the bats, and still I wake
at the shrill whistling, the flutter overhead.

I fumble to a tall window open among maples.
A car crawling a hill splashes my face with light
spread fine by mist that had been summer rain,
a sweetness that drips from black-palmed leaves.
The breeze I feel is damp, edged with mown hay,

enough to make me think the thumps and titters
I hear might be the loving pleasure of parents
unguessed, a long quarrel ended, a thrilling
touch that trails to muffled play. Slight shadows,
these are bats, residents of the house elders
built to last, the vaulted attic tall as a man

holding them hung in rows daylong like words
unuttered above the yard where children romp.
Flashlight in hand, I pass through the parlor
papered in silk for marriages the judge made,
and stand beneath the hidden door. The truth is

nothing can drive them out or contravene those
fretful, homespinning voices we cannot help
fearing as if they were the all-knowing dead.
Yet if I had one chair to stand tall enough on
I would climb with my light and shaking voice
to see whatever has lodged in their wizened eyes.

Under a room I have never seen but know, I stand
like one of the unblessed at the edge of dawn.
Smelling mold, I hear a dog's hopeless howl
and think of the stillness in the deep heads
of creatures who hang in sleep that is like love

in the children we cannot keep forever, absolute.
Each one near me unfurls a homekeeping song no
darkness or deed can kill. With them all green
from the field clings beyond each flood of light.
As if I had never been out of this room, I listen.
The sound is like rain, leaves, or sheets settling.

1983

Sea Owl

Unlike the hawk he has no dream of height,
his shadow is what he cannot remember.
In the wide and unlit room of the night
he waits. It is always December,

with the floor of the pines full of silver.
His toys move but his claws go tight
as soundlessly he descends the air.
Nothing knows his cradle, where the white

drone of the day hides him. The flesh-bright
ribbons tear in his grip. He dismembers
the shore's secrets. The iron-spike
of the sun is all he remembers.

1983

WRECK IN THE WOODS

Under that embrace of wild saplings held fast,
surrounded by troops of white mushrooms, by wrens
visiting like news-burdened ministers known
only to some dim life inside, this Model
A Ford like my grandfather's entered the earth.
What were fenders, hood, doors no one washed, polished,
grazed with a tip of finger, or boyhood dream?
I stood where silky blue above went wind-rent,
pines, oaks, dogwood ticking, pushing as if grief
called families to see what none understood. What
plot of words, what heart-shudder of men, women
here ended so hard the green world must hide it?
Headlights, large, round. Two pieces of shattered glass.

1996

MAKING A STATEMENT

Thousands, lately, have asked me about my hair.
Why is it so long? Why haven't you cut it?
I think about Samson, of course, and his woe.
His hair like thickets where I was born, swamps,
tall grasses bending with red-winged blackbirds
near a woman's nipples in the quick sun-gold.
I could tell about Samson, about the girl,
but I say my head is cold. I need cover.
Playing tennis with a leggy blonde I love,
I admit I can't do anything with it, my youth.
She rolls her eyes into a smashing serve.
"You old guys," she sighs with her drop shot.
Back and forth all day, yellow balls, long gray hair.

2002

Nance Van Winckel

Nance Van Winckel was born in Roanoke, Virginia, in 1951. She received her MA degree from the University of Denver. Although her earlier poetry frequently relied upon a strong narrative thread, her recent poems have a more ruminative, lyrical quality. To put it another way, she tends to use narrative to center a poem around an event rather than give poems a story-like quality. She has published four collections of poetry, *Bad Girl, With Hawk; The Dirt; After a Spell;* and *Beside Ourselves,* as well as three collections of short stories, *Limited Lifetime Warranty; Quake;* and *Curtain Creek Farm.* A recipient of NEA grants, the Washington Governor's Award for literature, and other awards, Van Winckel currently teaches in the MFA programs at Eastern Washington University and Vermont College.

Basket with Blue Ox

for Donna

Today it seems plausible that myth alone could
have made this place, or made it possible
at least for us to be here, this small lake
where once the great woodsman stepped,
drunkenly, on his way home. Cross-legged
on the dock, we weave baskets of willow,
mulberry root, small nests we dip again
and again into the cool water. Only here
could everything the past imagined for us
seem true: how spring is a single season,
that it somehow makes us tender. Or that
the blue ox lies down each night on the far
shore and wakes with a breath that blows off
morning's fog. In their unsinkable boats
our husbands fish close to that shore
as we continue these baskets, fill them
with stories. Our friend the loon listens
to tale after tale; his cries of belief detonate
on the still air. Today the preposterous lies
line up in our baskets on the dock.
We have made them and there is no limit
to what they can hold. The lake is nothing less
than the footprint of a man, these baskets the honor
of hopeful hands, and men in boats must come back,
ushering in the dark, carrying beautiful fishes.

1988

NICHOLAS BY THE RIVER

Two heaps of clothes by an old stump,
and Nicholas neck-deep in the water
too cold for our own good. Shimmering
when he said he wasn't sure but thought
maybe it was a man he wanted,
though I was what he had
under his hands in that blue current—
darker and rougher in the middle
over the deep spots. Nearly the end
of eighteen, and too late in August not
to expect even that which I'd been denied.

Upriver a couple hundred yards
an old man dropped his hook & sinker
and was already watching it drift away
when he saw us—our pair of heads
like two white rocks at the river's edge.
So nothing need have gone much
further. No one need have groped
in the furious currents, or the lovely lazy fish
have come to harm in our close proximity.

And I need not have taken my friend
around the craggy jut of rocks
and bent over him as he lay back
shivering in the sun. Maybe it was
not even necessary for him to moan a little
and turn me from him, bend me forward,
head down, hair dragging the water,
so he could enter me the only way
he knew, saying sorry sorry sorry.

1994

As is His Wont

He wants to be brought back to himself. To lose himself. He wants it to be still early in the history of the world. And to reside right here, in this instant of passion transubstantiating itself into yet another democratic crusade.

He wants to feel bad and be left alone. To revel in the damp of me, the rain of my body dripping down. He wants his own country to get its affairs in order, and to understand how it possibly could. Without him.

He wants it to be an hour with heat and electricity humming, so he won't have to feel his way down rain-slick streets to our dark hotel where I won't be able to explain the pluperfect, and we'll both lie here, sleepless and confused about what was love and what is loyalty, and all for some country that doesn't know its own borders or even what its name on the new map will be.

He wants me to witness the dual question marks of his shoulders walking away. To see him throw his hands down. To raise his hands up, as if to say Stop, stop. To shake out the shadows between our sentences and feel them drape. A cool on our heat. If only we could unload the dead fish from our dreams. If only what had been coming at us so fast—open-mouthed and already chewing—had frozen in its tracks, given us time to think it through, to think to think to think.

He wants back inside our endless passage: that processing of passion into its next declension. He wants the rain to quit. To have never begun. And for the sky to go on knotting and clenching, sending out spasms of voltage, thunder, coughs, contortions—before its fissure rips open and the downpour pours down.

2003

APPETITE, THE GREAT PAINTING

The vulture ravishes a rabbit. Gold talons
grip the ripped chest, where the heart—
gloriously stroked by a few hairs—
appears still beating.

This is a country's masterpiece. Hauled in
and out of secret subterranean tunnels.
A viewer goes up close. As we did. The torn middle
is a mystery. Wounds on wounds.

The forest: all eyes in the background.
As we were in the foreground. Marvelous:
the high moon that gives no light.
The bird's beak and claws make their own.

Half-closed, the eyes of the one eating
have the look of a lover, loving.

2003

The Avant-Garde

Behind a rail car warehouse, the bronze Lenins
with busted noses, missing chunks of feet. Ice
and pigeon shit on chipped mustaches. Five
headless torsos leaning every way at once.

And a girl tying one end of a jumprope
to half a hand. Taking her time. Looping
a noose up and over, testing the cinch,
her whole face the size of the halved palm.

She picks up her end. Gives it a few
slow turns. By her feet a pocked bronze eye
stares into the sun. She steps back a step.
Turns faster. Getting the right torque.

So all is perfected, though the day's still early,
the school bell not yet rung. The girl studies
the spin, whomps up the beat, already lost,
already singing what must be sung.

2003

Carolyne Wright

Carolyne Wright was born in Bellingham, Washington, in 1949. She has masters and doctoral degrees in English and Creative Writing from Syracuse University. Her books of poetry include *Premonitions of an Uneasy Guest, From a White Woman's Journal,* and, most recently, *Seasons of Mangoes and Brainfire,* winner of the Blue Lynx Prize and the American Book Award. She has also written a collection of essays, *A Choice of Fidelities: Lectures and Readings from a Writer's Life,* and translated three volumes of poetry from Spanish and Bengali. A widely traveled writer, Wright has also won a National Endowment for the Arts grant for her translation work which demonstrates the same acuity of vision and deft musicality found in her own poetry. After a number of visiting positions in creative writing and literature at colleges and universities throughout the U.S., Wright has recently returned to write and teach in her native Seattle.

KZ

"Arbeit Macht Frei"
—Motto over the entrance of every
Nazi concentration camp

We walk in under the empty tower, snow
falling on barbed-wire nets where the bodies
of suicides hung for days. We follow signs
to the treeless square, where the scythe blade, hunger,
had its orders, and some lasted hours in the cold
when all-night roll calls were as long as winter.

We've come here deliberately in winter,
field stubble black against the glare of snow.
Our faces go colorless in wind, cold
the final sentence of their bodies
whose only identity by then was hunger.
The old gate with its hated grillework sign

walled off, we take snapshots to sign
and send home, to show we've done right by winter.
We've eaten nothing, to stand inside their hunger.
We count, recount crimes committed in snow—
those who sheltered their dying fellows' bodies
from the work details, the transport trains, the cold.

Before the afternoon is gone, the cold
goes deep, troops into surrendered land. Signs
direct us to one final site, where bodies
slid into brick-kiln furnaces all winter
or piled on iron stretchers in the snow
like a plague year's random harvest. What hunger

can we claim? Those who had no rest from hunger
stepped into the ovens, knowing already the cold
at the heart of the flame. They made no peace with snow.

For them no quiet midnight sign
from on high—what pilgrims seek at the bottom of winter—
only the ebbing measure of their lives. Their bodies

are shadows now, ashing the footprints of everybody
who walks here, ciphers carrying the place of hunger
for us, who journey so easily in winter.
Who is made free by the merciless work of cold?
What we repeat when we can't read the signs—
the story of our own tracks breaking off in snow.

Snow has covered the final account of their bodies
but we must learn the signs: they hungered,
they were cold, and in Dachau it was always winter.

2000

MY LAST NIGHT IN BAHIA

I sat in the Mercado Modelo
drinking rum and pineapple,
waiting all afternoon on a promise—
Eric the Dutch poet, the self-
declared expatriate, gone AWOL
in eight languages from his country's
national service, refusing
to let me take his picture
on steps of the Bomfim church.

Was he casing shops in the square
where we'd danced all night
in crowds maddened by *cachaça*
and *samba* superstars
making love to their guitars
upon the Carnaval sound trucks?
Was he back at the hotel
where I'd followed once, where
he came down hours later with Gilsinha?

In the spendthrift sun of the market,
I watched *capoeira* players
turn their dream-slow cartwheels,
turbanned women call out
the responses, the *berimbáu*
moan on its one string.

I wore scarlet headscarves
and gold hoops in my ears,
lived on coffee and passion fruit,
street slang and the nervous
lassitude of the dancers.
I'd never fit in.

What lies did I tell myself
nights on my back in the driftwood-
littered sand of Porto da Barra?
The fisherman who stumbled over us
shaking his net-knife, shouting
"Pimp! Puta!" until we clambered
trembling, clutching our scattered
clothing, to our feet.

Salt grit between our thighs
all the way back in the streetcar,
cockfights and syncopated whistles
from the *samba* schools
pierced through my room's thin walls
as he thrust into me again
and again to finish what we'd started.

What about dawn's sudden gusts
of confetti, the clown suit
in a doorway during a sudden downpour
who grabbed Eric's beard and yelled
"Unmask!"?

My thoughts were too far gone.
What did the conjure woman tell me
when the glare from the glass ball
shone on her face through cigarette smoke?
Was it a blessing or a curse?
When the spell wore off
I stumbled alone down Ash Wednesday's
abandoned, trash-filled streets.

Then Celso da Costa was beside me—
quiet, slim, the West Coast
of Africa in his skin.
Celso the sidewalk artist
on the outskirts of our little group.

People stared at us as we danced
the circle *samba.*
"Who expects them to understand?"

He offered his parents' house
for the night, no need to explain
what no one can pay back to another.
A pink stucco cottage behind the square,
blue doors to keep out the bad eye,
sweet herbs in the garden.
One long whitewashed room,
pictures of saints on the walls.

I was ashamed of my hesitation.
After beans and rice and oranges
they gave me the one big bed,
Celso and his brothers on the floor,
his parents behind the kitchen curtain.
The night returning me to myself,
I emptied my pouches of conjure powders.

In the morning, the early bus
back to Rio, and Celso gave me
a painting—a house with blue shutters,
a garden, a dark-skinned family
waving goodbye in the doorway,
their faces full of what
almost could have kept me.

2000

The Peace Corps Volunteer Comes Home

Carrying the Kodak prints
she sent, her parents meet her
at the depot: What has she made
of the Third World?

The answer comes to her
like marked money—Brasil's
old joke: *"Café e Pelé."*
The principle exports.
She doesn't mention the color
of her lover's hands.

Her mother wrote, "Bring home
the coffee, nothing but the coffee."
She's a big girl now, she brings home
the rhythm, *Orfeo Negro*
in her walk. Her gray eyes
darkening in equatorial light.

At the Steak 'N' Ale, *feijoada*
lingers on her tongue. She waves away
the New York cut. *Recife*, she says,
Safety Zone. Good roads, and machetes
working through the cane.

Father nods,
turns off the burglar alarms
in his thoughts. Mother brings out
the china pattern, shows
what she's added.

Neither wants to know their daughter
sleeps in the other world, dreams
in the passion flower's language,

balancing the unbroken promise
of a man's body
against her, carrying the love child,
silence, like a *figa* charm.

2000

POST-REVOLUTIONARY LETTER

After cities full of flashbacks and bad debts,
you send me a letter from a country
safely out of reach,
your get-even scorecard: Love
or nothing.
                    Should I wish myself
into your place? You rented a room
above the gun-runners' bar,
fumes of *chicha* and kerosene
through floorboards, men in shirtsleeves
hunched over tables in a low room,
their tongues loosened by Molotov cocktails
and the jokes you could be shot
on sight for telling.

You shuffled a stacked deck,
spent hours dialing area codes
of fallen countries, friends
who disappeared in unmarked cars
before dawn. You say you want me again
but everything has its price.
                    Memory lapses,
hands losing their nerve, fingers
pointing to the *Keep Out* signs,
telling us whom to hate.
Were you always in the vanguard,
with a cause you could get strangers
to believe in? Did you wonder
how you got there, when fireworks
strafed the night sky, and amputees
from the last war crawled under benches?

In the duty-free shops, vodka
dropped like mercury in the bottles.
Rifles filled the crates marked *Shoes*,
and bribed inspectors whistled,
looking out across winter hills.

The years are worn out
by forwarding addresses, everything I said
twisted by your dictum—*Don't Look Back*.
I put your letter down.
I won't be at the airport
listening to doctored radio reports
and making out with the taxi driver
till you arrive.

2000

SIERRA WALK

(Ollantaitambo, Perú)

I stepped off the Cuzco-Machu
Picchu local, and the thin air
reeled with constellations.
I asked the way to town.
The station master swung his oil lamp
and our smudged faces
flickered on its panes.

No, he didn't know the roads,
the platform's widening rings
of dark. He never held in mind
what dropped away over the edges
of a city woman's sight.
"But this *cholita*"—he pointed
to a shape bend under bundles
and layers of shawls—"can take you.
They all know the way."

The woman assented in a warble
high and strange as a candle
flickering in a mountain shrine.
She turned and walked.
I took my pack and followed.

The Inca woman trudged ahead
on the rutted *llama* track,
her silence dark and tightly braided.
Above us, eucalyptus limbs
held up the night.

Other shapes fell in behind,
stocky and silent as my guide.
I shifted the pack's unbalanced load,
shrank into layers of my own dark.
Among forms that fit the path
—like priests in whatever road
their god guides them—I had to save
myself from stumbling.

Oil lamps in windows
fixed our silhouettes. The road
turned into town. In the square
the crowd disbanded, lamps
went down like lids.
The Inca woman moved up the mountain
to her hut of fitted stone.

I moved alone through the streets,
speechless, dark as faces
extinguished under shawls,
trying to empty myself of all names
and summon the courage
to knock on windowless plank doors
and ask the blank-faced dwellers for a room.

2000

Robert Wrigley

Robert Wrigley was born in East St. Louis, Illinois in 1951. In 1976, he earned an MFA degree from the University of Montana, where he studied with Richard Hugo. The author of six books of poetry, including *Moon in a Mason Jar*, *What My Father Believed*, *In the Bank of Beautiful Sins*, *Reign of Snakes*, and *Lives of Animal*, Wrigley is a celebrated and original poet. The recipient of Guggenheim and Kingsley Tufts Awards, as well as many others, Wrigley writes dramatic and musically propelled poetry, combining narrative threads with a percussive attention to the sonic texture of his poetry. Rooted in a firm sense of place—whether the Midwest of his origins or the Idaho of his mature life—his poems articulate awareness and passion. Wrigley is currently a professor in the creative writing program at the University of Idaho.

THE SKULL OF A SNOWSHOE HARE

I found it in the woods, moss-mottled,
hung at the jaws by a filament
of leathery flesh. We have painted it
with Chlorox, bleached it
in that chemical sun, boiled loose
the last tatters of tissue,
and made of it an heirloom,
a trophy, a thing that lasts, death's
little emissary to an eight-year-old boy.

What should it mean to us now
In its moon-white vigil on the desk?
Light from the hallway makes it loom
puffball brilliant, and I look.
For no good reason but longing
I am here in your room,
straightening the covers, moving a toy,
and lightly stroking your head,
those actions I have learned to live by.

If we relish the artifacts of death,
it's for a sign that life goes on
without us. On the mountain snows
we've seen the hare's limited hieroglyphics,
his signature again and again
where we've skied. And surely
he has paused at our long tracks there,
huddled still as moonlight, and tested
for our scents long vanished in that air.

We live and die in what we have left.
For all the moon glow of that bone
no bigger than your fist, there is more
light in the way I touch you

when you're sleeping: the little electric sparks
your woolen blankets make clear
to my hand in the half-light,
and this page, white as my bones, and alive.

1986

MOON IN A MASON JAR

It was what you might as well wish for,
blue-in-the-face, pipe-dreamer.
Money taunts, another year
is gone by and still you're in that old coat,
those over-hauled dresses, your face
hand-tooled to a frown
while you dun by phone the other bad debtors.

Rue the day the fourth child was born,
rue worse the day it started.
Your hands are crabbed in wash water,
nails ravaged. And there is no sense
in happiness despite it all,
no glad release when, sweat-soaked,
you stack the last jar of fruit
on the pantry shelves and stand back to see them,
the yolky peaches, wine cherries,
the cool lunar lobes of the pears,
and the accompaniment each lid makes
as it pings and seals itself tight.

1986

WHAT MY FATHER BELIEVED

Man of his age, he believed in the things
built by men, the miracles of rockets and bombs,
of dams and foundries, the mind-killing
efficiency of assembly lines. And now the boredom
and blankness with which these students respond
to the tale of my father's loss of faith sadden me,
as times before I have saddened myself. Around
the middle of his life, I baited him wildly,
hung in my room the poster of Malcolm X,
whose lips were stilled around a word
that could have been freedom, or fight, or fuck.
I remember the first time I heard
my father say it. We had argued and I thought
I'd won. It was the same awful subject,
the war. I see now it was never how he had fought,
but his countrymen. He said we should not expect
to love war, but to know sometimes there was no way
around it, and I laughed and said, "Just stop."
In his eyes I saw what he couldn't say,
though right as I was, I could not
predict what he muttered. The rage that made
him flush and stutter and sweat was gone,
and only a fool of twenty couldn't see the blade
of pain he suffered, and suffered all along.
What should I say to him today, when the truth
I was so eager to embrace is constantly told,
when the plainness of it rankles like a bad tooth
in our mouths and the students scold
us both as naïve and thoughtless. What of Custer?
they ask. What of racism? slavery? the inexorable theft
of every acre of native land? And I can muster

no answer they'll accept, but am left
at the end of class the argument's dull loser,
silent, contemplating the nature of instruction.
My father believed in the nation, I in my father,
a man of whom those students have not the slightest notion.

1991

Ashtray in the Snow

If I had been careful last December
I'd have stowed the pair of chairs and the stump
table under the studio, so that

today, as spring snow melts off the porch,
I would not see this faceted glass thing
emerge like a reef of ice from the white sea,

nor, for that matter, the great fractured mast
of last year's final cigar, lying athwart
a broken shard, its nub of ash a raven.

2002

LETTER TO A YOUNG POET

In the biographies of Rilke, you get the feeling
you also get now and then in the poems
that here, surely, is a man among the archetypes of all men
you'd rather hang than have notice your daughter.
And yet, how not to admire the pure oceanic illogic
of his arguments, those preposterous
if irremediable verities. It can't be helped. They're true.
And there's no other word for him, for whom sadness is
a kind of foreplay, for whom seduction
is the by-product of the least practical art there is.
Those titanic skills in language, the knack lacked by
every other lung-driven swimmer through the waters
of lexicon, in spite of the fierce gravities of all grammar
and the sad, utilitarian wallflowers of usage:
well, there you go, my half-assed angel, that's your challenge.
Beethoven believed he was homely too, but you
must understand: Rilke's tools you can pick up, every one
but the one they all share. Even Stevens,
who must have known an actuary or two and still for whom
the brown salt skin of order sang beyond and in the ache
of longing. And Celan, whose most terrible angels
rang him like a bell of rings. And Whitman,
the dandy of the cocked hat and tilted head himself,
the gentlest, the gentile jew, the jubilant lonely grubber
eyeing the grocery boy. Inside
them all, a man, if you could help it,
you would never consent to become,
except if only, just for once, you could be him.

2003

Acknowledgements:

KIM ADDONIZIO

"Gravity," and "Them." *Philosopher's Club*. BOA Editions, 1994.
"Beer, Milk, the Dog, My Old Man." *Jimmy & Rita*. BOA
    Editions, 1997.
"Night of the Living, Night of the Dead," and "Prayer." *Tell Me:
    Poems*. BOA Editions, 2000.

LINDA BIERDS

"Ritual for the Dead, Lake Sakami, Quebec, 1980." *Flights of the
    Harvest Mare*. Ahsahta Press: 1985.
"The Stillness, The Dancing." *The Stillness and the Dancing*.
    Henry Holt & Co.: 1988. Used by permission of the author.
"Memento of the Hours." *The Ghost Trio*. Henry Holt & Co.:
    1995. Used by permission of the author.
"Safe." *The Profile Makers*. Owl Publishing Co.: 1997.
"The Seconds." *The Seconds*. GP Putnam & Sons: 2001.

GILLIAN CONOLEY

"As in the Small Gaps Between Minutes" and "After." *Beckon*.
    Carnegie Mellon University Press: 1996.
"The World" and "Beauty and the Beast." *Lovers in the Used World*.
    Carnegie Mellon University Press: 2001.
"New." *Profane Halo*. Verse Press: 2005.

Robert Hass

"Envy of Other People's Poems," "A Supple Wreath of Myrtle,"
"Futures in Lilacs," "Time and Materials" and "The World as
Will and Representation" are previously unpublished. Used by
permission of the author.

Brenda Hillman

"Adult Joy." *Bright Existence*. Wesleyan University Press: 1993.
"The Unbeginning" and "Cheap Gas." *Loose Sugar*. Wesleyan
University Press: 1997.
"Shared Custody" and "Pre-Uplift of the Sierra." *Cascadia*.
Wesleyan University Press: 2001.

Edward Hirsch

"And So It Begins Again." *For the Sleepwalkers*. Carnegie Mellon
University Press: 1998.
"Self-Portrait," "Boy With a Headset," "The Chardin Exhibition"
and "The History of My Stupidity: Volume 3, Chapter 5" used
by permission of the author.

Christopher Howell

"In the Spring of Hjalmar Carlson: The Real Story." *Sweet Afton*.
True Directions Press: 1991.
"The Bride of Long Division" and "The Christian Science
Minotaur." *Memory and Heaven*. Eastern Washington
University Press: 1996.
"He Writes to the Soul" and "The New Orpheus." *Light's Ladder*.
University of Washington Press: 2004.

Claudia Keelan

"Romanticism." *Refinery*. Cleveland State University Poetry
Center: 1994.
"The Secularist" and "The End is an Animal." *The Secularist*. The
University of Georgia Press: 1997.
"My Twentieth Century" and "Embers." *Utopic*. Alice James
Books: 2000.

Yusef Komunyakaa

"Let's Say." *Copacetic*. Wesleyan University Press: 1984.
"Starlight Scope Myopia." *Diem Cai Dau*. Wesleyan University Press: 1988.
"Once the Dream Begins," "Ambush," and "Urban Renewal." *Pleasure Dome: New and Collected Poems*. Wesleyan University Press: 2004.

Dorianne Laux

"What Could Happen." *American Poetry Review* 22.4 (July 1993): 13. Used by permission of the author.
"FireStarter," "Smoke," "Trying to Raise the Dead," and "Prayer." *Smoke: Poems*. BOA Editions: 2000.

Li-Young Lee

"The Gift," and "From Blossoms." *Rose*. BOA Editions: 1986.
"This Room and Everything In It" and "The Cleaving." *The City in which I love you*. BOA Editions: 1990.
"Eternal Son." *Book of My Nights*. BOA Editions: 2001.

Laura Mullen

"White Paintings, I-V." *After I Was Dead*. The University of Georgia Press: 1999.

Lucia Perillo

"The Destruction of the Mir." *The American Poetry Review* 31.1 (Jan/Feb 2002): 52.
"La Deuxieme Sexe," "Urban Legend," "Shrike Tree," and "For the Pileated Woodpecker and Its Cousin, the Ivory-Billed, Who May or May Not Be Extinct." *The American Poetry Review* 31.5 (Oct/Nov 2002): 25-27.
Used by permission of the author.

BIN RAMKE

"Like Ulysses" and "Art, Love, Geology." *Massacre of the Innocent.* University of Iowa Press: 1995.

"Enter Celia, with a Writing" and "Famous Poems of the Past Explained." *Wake.* University of Iowa Press: 1999.

"Thou Hast Blessed the Work of My Hands." *Matter.* University of Iowa Press: 2004

DONALD REVELL

"How Passion Came to Matter." *New Dark Ages.* Wesleyan University Press: 1990.

"Last." *Erasures.* Wesleyan University Press: 1992.

"Lyre." *Beautiful Shirt.* Wesleyan University Press: 1994.

"Fewer than Music." *There Are Three.* Wesleyan University Press: 1998.

"Toombs 4." *Arcady.* Wesleyan University Press: 2002.

DAVID ST. JOHN

"The Opal Tree," "Saffron," "After Esenin," and "Elegy," are previously unpublished. Used by permission of the author.

"Zuni Ring" is previously unpublished in book form. It appears at the Blackbird website; *http://www.blackbird.vcu.edu/v1n1/ poetry/stjohn_d/zuni.htm.*

DAVE SMITH

"The Dream of the Jacklighter," "Bats" and "Seal Owl." *In the House of Judge.* Carnegie Mellon Univ Press, 2004. Used by permission of the author.

"Making a Statement," and "Wreck in the Woods." *Fate's Kite: Poems 1991-1995.* Louisiana State University Press: 1996. Used by permission of the author.

Nance Van Winckel

"Basket With Blue Ox." *Bad Girl, with Hawk.* University of Illinois Press: 1988.

"Nicolas by the River." *The Dirt.* Miami University Press: 1994.

"The Avant-garde," "As Is His Wont," and "Appetite: The Great Painting." *Beside Ourselves.* Miami University Press: 2003.

Carolyne Wright

"My Last Night in Bahia," "Sierra Walk," "Post Revolutionary Letter," "KZ," and "The Peace Corps Volunteer Comes Home." *Season of the Mangoes and Brainfire.* Lynx House Press: 2000.

Robert Wrigley

"The Skull of a Snowshoe Hare," "Moon in a Mason Jar," and "What My Father Believed." *Moon in a Mason Jar* and *What my Father Believed.* University of Illinois Press: 1997.

"Ashtray in the Snow" and "Letter to a Young Poet" are previously unpublished. Used by permission of the author.